MW01127390

1st Edition

THE ABC's
OF
DIVERSITY:
Basic Workplace Communication

Leon T. Lanier, Sr.

The ABC's of Diversity: Basic Workplace Communication. Copyright 2005 by
Renaissance Books, Incorporated. All Rights Reserved.

Printed in the United States of America. No part of this book may be used or
reproduced in any manner whatsoever except in the case of brief quotations
embodied in critical articles and reviews.

For more information contact: Renaissance Books, Inc.,

ISBN No. 0-9662711-4-9

www.LanierDiversityConsultants.com
www.LanierDiversityBookstore.com

Renaissance
Publishers,
Inc.

INTRODUCTION

In our ever-changing society, there are many culturally-related perspectives that truly warrant our attention. This special introduction attempts to acknowledge those perspectives and how they silently affect the introspective growth and path-forward reality of an organization's diversity strategies. With this in mind, please be open-minded to the learning opportunities noted in…

"THE REVELATIONS OF THE EXCLUSIONARY MAN"

I began to acknowledge cultural differences after certain of my intuitions just didn't feel right anymore. I devalued this introspection because culture change, inclusion, and respect had already become flashing "buzz" words for several supposedly oppressed communities at my workplace.

Since my recent discovery about cultural difference issues, I've noticed that these same supposedly oppressed communities tended not to be their same old selves. They now communicate with other communities differently. They now interpret things differently. And, they now seek "equality rights" I never knew they had.

I will admit, however, I still expect certain attitudes when I'm forced to interact with them. Yet, some of those attitudes have vanished. Those people, as I at times say, have graduated to a more positive and expressive location of self.

Apparently, a new social mindset has grown in America that surrounds my every move – at home and at the office. Exactly who's lost? I really don't know. The responsibility of addressing culture change, or even suspecting change, belongs to whom? Again, I really don't know. The ideal proactive culture now becomes… that cluster of folks "over there" - a truth that, introspectively speaking, needs more personal work on my part.

The more I humble myself into respecting that cluster's worldview, the easier it is to persuade myself to accept their new worldview needs. To sort of acquiesce to the new establishment while still saving face… a fact very dear to my ego!

My mindset will eventually accept the world as it wants to be accepted. It will eventually accept you for whom you respectfully wish to be. And, it already accepts me for whom I am – biases and all – regardless of what any of "those other people" might be saying behind my back.

My reality of thought, a non-judgmental right or wrong, places me in a safe environment. It places me in an environment where, throughout the night, I don't have to stare at the moon and wonder how I fit into all of this culture identity "stuff."

How to address my workplace bias is not a part of my dreams. I will awaken with pretty much the same culture I put to sleep the night before. I feel very much at home here in my heart, no surprises. As I enter the workplace the next morning, I will carry with me a hidden diversity of thought, my biases, and a non-essential need to respectfully acknowledge the cultural lens of co-workers.

Cross-cultural competence is constantly being suggested by leaders as a path forward strategy. But, "Why can't I just be the real me?" I'm constantly being told "It's okay to be where I am. That my cultural lens was developed by my ethnocentric experiences. And, that my worldview allows me to explain my value in this everyday existence." If these statements are correct...

"Why should I take on this culture change journey?"
"Is it something I owe to corporate loyalty?" Or,
"Is it something I owe to a man-made conscience?"

The short answer may be that culture change will occur whether I like it or not. I think history has shown that culture change is, has been and always will be the way of the world. Those opposing it may awaken one morning and find themselves on a lonely island of insensitivity.

Earlier it was mentioned that, at times, "things just didn't feel right to me." Was that because even though I have freedom of choice, there's only one right decision in regard to accepting change? Am I struggling culturally because "I'm not doing the right thing?" Only time will tell.

During the months ahead, I ignored diversity policies and practices as fast as they were approved by top management. Yes, a revelation or two, however small, did make sense to me every now and then. But none caused me to scratch my head and truly think about how they impacted my existence.

At the workplace, newly hired employees were replacing my peers in number and in mindset. Water cooler conversations spoken in different tongues had different meanings, and client bases expanded to those "of the future" instead of those from the past.

A bottom-line business case revelation was upon me. What am I to do? How do I sustain my part in this culturally changing world? I thought my valued longevity within the status quo would carry me until the end of my career. The end as I knew it and not through the non-inclusive eyes of another. A second revelation to me indeed!

Visiting my client base has become more and more uncomfortable. A telephone call used to satisfy brand and client loyalty. The brand is still the same but loyalty now means more to the new user. It now means more to the new user who no longer looks just like me. It means more to the *new user who is exercising an economic reality to gain greater respect in the marketplace. Sure. I knew this demographic fact was coming... but, didn't know when. It's here and I'm not prepared to deal with it.*

Current leadership is open to only one thing – including the new market's cultural reality in the mix. My level of effectiveness is directly tied to new market acquisitions and renewals. Metrics supporting this business direction are strong and are ones I cannot deny. I'm having trouble identifying with my old customer's fast changing workforce. Is this another dark revelation? You can bet your life on it. But, it's too early to retire. I still have to work for a living!

The company has been telling me year after year that I needed to "re-invent" myself. That I needed to re-invest in "me" as my own human capital investment. That I needed to change my mindset to one of respect, inclusion, and open-mindedness of other cultures. To "reach out and touch" something foreign to the cultural workplace norms of yesteryear. In even more of a commitment, the company wants me to expand my ethnocentric beliefs and values by honestly acknowledging ethnocentric beliefs and values of others. Now... "ain't" that an ethnorelative mountain to ask an old, loyal employee to climb (pardon the English)?

The workplace is surely not fair at times. Certain previous ideologies are no longer acceptable. I can't simply show up and be valued for who I am anymore. My worth is based on who I can now become. The responsibility to affect organizational growth is diminishing for my elite group of workforce dinosaurs. And, speaking of dinosaurs, didn't they rule the Earth at one time or another? Change wasn't friendly to them either.

Maybe I need to have a straight talk with myself? I'm still loyal to the company. I'm still loyal to the workplace that sent my kids to college. I'm still loyal to our corporate vision and our ever-changing mission statement. So, "Why do I feel betrayed? Why is it now "my" responsibility to change? Why did the company let me down by not solidifying our place in the world's global market? Didn't they see this era of globalization coming? Didn't they know the world was shrinking? How did our leaders miss the future value to be placed on women and minorities? What about cross-cultural competence and what it stands for?" Culture change must be about that almighty dollar. If it is, it too shall soon pass... I hope.

On a more personal note, my grandchild is such a blessed person. All the credit belongs to his wonderful parents even though we rarely agree on how to properly raise him. He's 10 years old and one of the best things to happen in my life. I agreed to observe his first elementary school play and to finally meet his precious little Sally. He has a young crush on this little lady and she's supposed to star in the school's production. I can't wait to meet her.

The school's play was a hit although I never did recognize the Sally who commanded my grandson's attention. Shortly after it concluded, I felt a little tug on my jacket. I turned around only to see my cute little grandson standing there with an embarrassed, shy grin on his face. Next to him stood his precious little Sally – a sweet child… "of color"… and quite different than anyone I thought my grandson should be involved with relationship-wise. I tried to remain calm but my facial messages apparently said enough for his little mind. He grabbed Sally's hand and quietly rushed her away.

Several weeks later, he finally asked me what was wrong with Sally. I had no response. I did, however, embarrassingly recognize that I had shipwrecked myself on that deserted island of cultural insensitivity. I felt so alone at that time.

During this culturally insensitive acknowledgement, a first ever "Aha!" entered my mind. My resistance to another's cultural worldview had become apparent in the most harshness of ways – through the eyes of a 10 year old child. Ownership of my bias was now necessary more than ever before.

Secretly driven by my embarrassing "Aha!" discovery, I decided to learn how to become more open-minded both socially and professionally. I decided to reach out and touch another's culture without broadcasting my ignorance to their cultural truths.

Since reaching out for understanding, I feel so much better about my current self. Yet, unfortunately, I still can't forget that inquisitive lesson gleaming from my grandson's *"inclusive" eyes! I don't wish that on anyone.*

How did I ever get to this place? What were the warning signs of change? How could I not recognize them? Come to think of it, several obvious warning signals did actually exist….. "the changing workplace, the changing customer base, and my unchanging mindset!"

Are there any "revelations" in your organization?

As you embark on your personal journey to cross-cultural competence, you must remember to not only take ownership of your worldviews, but develop confidence in how to communicate those worldviews when cultural learning opportunities exist. The "ABC's of Diversity: Basic Workplace Communication" can support this "personal work" by introducing a consistent, culture-based terminology into your specific environment. The opportunity to affect this action is yours to give.

- *Leon T. Lanier, Sr.*

CONTENTS

xiv

xvii

THE ABC'S
OF
DIVERSITY
:Basic Workplace Communication

Renaissance Publishers, Inc.

The ABC's of Diversity:

Acceptance

o o o

Acceptance, in a cultural worldview context, has been analyzed by Dr. Milton Bennett and Dr. Michael Hammer's Developmental Model of Intercultural Sensitivity (DMIS) and is measured by its Intercultural Development Inventory instrument (IDI). Within this context, being in acceptance "suggests that you acknowledge and respect cultural difference. When you think of people from other cultures, you imagine them as every bit as complex as yourself. Their ideas, feelings, and behavior may seem unusual to you, but you realize that their experience is just as rich as your own. You might not like everything about the other cultures (or everything about your own, for that matter) but that fact does not make you think that any cultural group is more or less civilized. You are curious about other cultures and seek opportunities to learn more about them, even if you do not have many opportunities to interact with members of those cultures.

As an example, if you are traveling or living in other cultures, you may not act any differently than you do with members of your own culture. But you are probably aware that your behavior might be interpreted in unusual ways.

Basic Words of Communication

The ABC's of Diversity:

You, in turn, are probably careful to withhold quick judgments of members of other cultures and to consider how their behavior might mean something different than it would in your own culture."

1-(Excerpt from the Developmental Model of Intercultural Sensitivity's Intercultural Development Inventory Manual by Dr. Mitch Hammer and Dr. Milton Bennett, 1998).

(1) Based on this cultural definition, how accepting are you of other cultures?

(2) Are your social and workplace attitudes similar when it comes to how you interact to cultural difference?

ACCEPTING
BIASES

o o o

No Fault...No Blame

Accepting the biases of others requires a very open and honest introspection. The bottom-line is that we must respect and value the voices of others regardless of their individual worldviews. Each of us has our own set of ethnocentric experiences – experiences that helped shape our

Basic Words of Communication

present character and thought process. There should be no fault, no blame, and certainly no shame attached to where we currently find ourselves and others in this life.

We have no exact replica of us in this world. No other person has walked in our shoes. The only qualities known about us are those that are assumed and those we've intentionally shared with others. Thus, no one knows the real value we place on cultural sensitivity.

In many instances, we aren't aware we possess particular biases. Once new biases have been brought to our attention, we need time to acknowledge ownership and to respond to them.

Evaluate your personal history. If you discover you hadn't handled a bias toward another in a more sensitive manner, please note that change in yourself may not occur overnight. However, eliminating finger pointing or blaming is a good start towards respect. If you have a history of unfairly addressing examples of workplace bias, just ask yourself why? The answer can be discovered if you are honest with yourself. Candid conversations and sharing of experiences can help your maturity in this regard.

(1) List several biases you would like your organization to address from a leadership role;

(2) From an individual contributor's perspective.

ACCEPTING CHANGE

o o o

What Causes Workplace Change?

Our expanding world is in a constant state of change. Corporate loyalty is aligned more and more with bottom-line profits instead of the employee's well-being. Life-long job assignments that promised pension benefits are no longer guaranteed. Automation reproduces widgets many times faster than any human effort. Therefore, workplace norms as we know them can change in a heartbeat.

Competition mandates implementation of more efficient work strategies. To keep up with this implementation, we must choose to rededicate ourselves to new commitments, new ideologies, and newly defined workplace values – our own as well as those espoused by the organization. We must teach ourselves how to individually embrace the consequences of change and how best to introduce them into our social arena. Change will take place whether you want it to or not. Be mentally proactive about it.

(1) What workplace behaviors would you like to enhance as a leader?

(2) As an individual contributor?

Basic Words of Communication

ACCEPTING PERSONAL OWNERSHIP

o o o

Why Is It So Difficult?

Personal ownership is nothing more than being true to your mindset. It's very hard to accept personal biases, verbal and non-verbal shortcomings, and/or to acknowledge a need to improve in certain culturally sensitive domains. Lacking personal ownership makes it difficult to accept questionable evaluations from supervisors who don't really know you. Lacking personal ownership also makes it difficult to look in the mirror and accept that, because your production is not what it used to be, the company doesn't want you around anymore.

The situation becomes even more complicated observing younger, lesser-deserved employees getting promoted all around you. It's difficult to lead by example when a decision may negatively affect a close acquaintance. It's difficult to make decisions based on merit. And, it's difficult to close your eyes to negative workplace stereotypes.

Yet, to find the heart, strength, and character to accept these conditions - as reality - is a good example of what constitutes accepting personal ownership.

The ABC's of Diversity:

Accepting personal ownership allows you to make sound decisions and to live with the consequences. Personal ownership mandates a "walk-the-talk" personality. Personal ownership welcomes risk taking and allows you to stretch your comfort zone and invite others to follow your lead. And, last but not least, personal ownership, in its purest form, allows you to sleep at night.

Challenge your commitment to accepting personal ownership. Share an example of a personal bias you never before dared to share…
(1) As a leader?

(2) As an individual contributor?

ACCOUNTABILITY

o o o

What It Means In The Workplace?
Accountability may be the most sought after value associated to workplace change. Accountability is taking responsibility for your actions whether they are personal, professional, or psychological.

Basic Words of Communication

The ABC's of Diversity:

On the employee side, I think employees prefer to define accountability as owning up to a realistic value they can bring to an organization. Trading the positives they can instill for that which they can be compensated. Sounds simple enough but is it really?

Employee accountability should go a bit further. It should enhance one's personal motivation to always bring his or her best self to the workplace. Employee accountability should seek to naturally practice policies of inclusion without the pressure of corporate mandates and to value cultural differences both inside and outside of the corporate walls.

Leaders may define accountability as "showing the way so others may follow." Leaders should implement policies and procedures for a corporate direction along with accepted consequences. Leaders should demonstrate the character and honesty they would demand from others. And, true leaders should always "do the right thing" regardless of public opinion.

How does a leader espouse to these values? How does a leader tell his executives to place a value on diversity and inclusion practices even at the expense of profitability when a reduction of either may be an automatic loss of job? How does a leader tie diversity measurements to annual paychecks, then not honor those measurements based on a very positive profit/loss statement? These questions are true questions of accountability.

Accountability means a lot of things to a lot of people. It definitely demands self-sacrifice from leaders and individual contributors to honor the policies and procedures of the organization. Accountability is simply doing what you said you would do and letting the consequences fall where they may. Thus, as stated earlier, sounds simple enough but is it really?

How is accountability valued in your organization...

(1) At the leadership level?

(2) At the Individual contributor level?

———

ACKNOWLEDGING WORKPLACE FEAR

o o o

Why is it important?

Exactly what is the gap between the true workplace perception and employee reality? When your supervisors place an evaluation form in front of you and ask that you "honesty" respond to the instrument, "How honest can you actually be?" Loyalty to the company is very important. Are you really going to use this opportunity to admit to an unhappy workplace environment? And, if you dare do so, what are the perceived repercussions?

In a book entitled "Driving Fear out of the Workplace: Creating the High Trust – High Performance Organization by Kathleen Ryan and Daniel Oestreich," it says that "workplace fear cannot be changed into trust unless organizational leaders consciously decide to behave in ways that will turn around negative workplace patterns. To do this, it is recommended that you start with yourself. As you increase your personal understanding and its impact, two things must happen. First, you will be better positioned to help others build that same awareness. Second, your proactive leadership in acknowledging fear's presence will serve as a model for others in the organization.

The ABC's of Diversity:

You can further enhance this process if you:
(1) Learn from your own experiences with workplace fears by reflecting on times you wanted to speak on a topic but hesitated to do so;

(2) Discuss the sensitive subjects connected to fear in the workplace;

(3) Resist getting caught up in the cycle of mistrust by learning how to deal with issues of anger, cynicism, complaining, labeling, an apparent resistance to moving forward; and,

(4) Seek clarity about your style and your performance by asking for, understanding, and then responding to feedback."

Don't hesitate to enhance this process by enlisting the support of other managers who report to you. You can do this by: (1) sharing your reasons for wanting to reduce fear and build trust in the organization; (2) explore their concerns about your action plan; and (3), use a checklist of the possible symptoms and costs of fear such as lawsuits, poor customer service, bad decisions, and unethical behavior etc.
24(Driving Fear out of the Workplace: Creating the High Trust - High Performance Organization by Kathleen Ryan and Daniel Oestreich, pg 131)

Are there any hidden fears in your workplace environment?

Basic Words of Communication

The ABC's of Diversity:

ADAPTATION

o o o

Adaptation, in a cultural worldview context as described by the Intercultural Development Inventory (IDI), is explained as both a Cognitive Frame-Shifting form of Adaptation and as a Behavioral Code-Shifting form of Adaptation. Resolved issues in the Cognitive Frame-Shifting form indicate that you recognize the added value of having more than one cultural perspective available to you. Furthermore, you are able to "take the perspective" of another culture for the purpose of understanding or evaluating situations in either your or another's culture. An example would be that "if you are not bi-cultural, you probably would like to be, if you had the opportunity."

Resolved issues in the Behavior Code-Shifting form of Adaptation indicate that you are able to intentionally change your culturally-based behavior. You have a broad repertoire of behavior that allows you to act in culturally appropriate ways outside your own culture. For instance: As a businessperson, you are likely to be accomplished in negotiations across cultures or managing multicultural teams. You may often find yourself facilitating intercultural discussions.
3-(taken from the Intercultural Development Inventory Manual by Dr. Mitch Hammer and Dr. Milton Bennett, 1998).

List several ethnocentric experiences that helped you mature and develop your skills in adaptation.

Basic Words of Communication

ADULT LEARNING

o o o

Workplace Definition?

Adult learning can be defined as the development of educational processes and delivery strategies as they apply to adult learners identified in a specific workplace environment. This development also requires acknowledging the maturity factor of the participants, the pace of the delivered instruction, and the educational aptitude levels previously inherited by the participant.

4- Kathleen Ryan & Daniel Ostreich; Driving Fear out of the Workplace: Creating a High Trust High Performance Organization; Second Edition, pg 129; Jossey-Bass, 1998.

AFFINITY GROUPS

o o o

An affinity group is a group of people or a specific segment of any environment that wishes to share a common interest, background, or goal. The power of such a group is its ability to enhance its "voice and concerns" throughout the

Basic Words of Communication

organization in an effort to remain inclusive to corporate policies and practices.

(1) Name such groups in your environment and evaluate their workplace value.

(2) Are they officially recognized in the organization?

AFFIRMATIVE ACTION

o o o

My Definition…

Affirmative action is a term used to describe special efforts to recruit and employ individuals from groups that have been historically and systematically disadvantaged. Affirmative action is designed to correct under-utilization of qualified women and minorities.

The ABC's of Diversity:

Workplace Perception?

This term has several perceptions - all of which are valuable. The first perception is one where mandated litigation by America's judicial system pressured for overall fairness in the workplace. The next perception is that affirmative action is nothing more than a legal process that authorizes decision-makers to make sure under-qualified participants are fairly represented in specific workforce communities. And, another perception of affirmative action focuses on the strength of the exclusion term … "reverse discrimination."

The key here is to enhance the awareness of each perception and how these perceptions affect the mindset of all individual contributors in the organization. Each employee must have a better understanding of where he or she is personally on this definition before positive movement can be made. Communication is vital.

How is affirmative action perceived by mindsets in your organization?

(1) At the individual contributor level?

(2) At the Leadership level?

Basic Words of Communication

AGE
DISCRIMINATION
IN
EMPLOYMENT ACT
OF
1967

○ ○ ○

This Age Discrimination in Employment Act is federal legislation that bans employers of 20 or more workers from firing or refusing to hire an individual 40 to 65 years of age simply because of age – unless age is a bona fide job qualification; forbids employment agencies to refuse to refer a job applicant because of age and to indulge in other discriminatory practices. Violators of the law face penalties.

This act was amended in 1978, raising from 65 to 70 the age at which an employer can require workers to retire involuntarily.

AMERICAN CULTURE

o o o

How is it Different?

"Americans think of themselves as individuals first, view the world as basically inanimate and nature as something to be conquered, and consider material success as the major goal and "doing" as the preferred state. Most value self-improvement and hard work as the way to ensure a better future for themselves and their families."

"Americans believe in scientific and technological progress and view the world in rational, linear, cause and effect terms. People from other cultures usually see Americans as pragmatic, factual, and future oriented, with a tendency to view things in either-or terms rather than the shades between."

5-(taken from Diversity Success Strategies, Chapter 2, pg 34, written by Norma-Carr Ruffino, Butterworth/Heinemann Publishers, 1999)

The ABC's of Diversity:

AMERICANS
WITH
DISABILITIES
ACT
OF
1990

ooo

Title I of the <u>Americans with Disabilities Act of 1990</u> prohibits private employers, state and local governments, employment agencies and labor unions from discriminating against qualified individuals with disabilities in job application procedures, hiring, firing, advancement, compensation, job training, and other terms, conditions, and privileges of employment. The ADA covers employers with 15 or more employees, including state and local governments. It also applies to employment agencies and to labor organizations. The ADA's nondiscrimination standards also apply to federal sector employees under section 501 of the Rehabilitation Act, as amended, and its implementing rules. An individual with a disability is a person who: (1) has a physical or mental impairment that substantially limits one or more major life activities; (2) has a record of such an impairment; or (3) is regarded as having such an impairment.

Basic Words of Communication

ARCHETYPES

○ ○ ○

The tendency of a group or segment of people who are "of the same cultural background" to behave in a certain way. This differs from the definition of stereotype in that this term refers to a segment "within" a specific stereotyped group, while stereotype refers to the "entire" group.

ASSUMPTIONS

○ ○ ○

An assumption is the act of laying claim to or taking possession of something; an assuming that something is true; a fact or statement taken for granted; a belief of what others believe or feel founded on non-direct information.

Make a list of five assumptions you had of others in your workplace environment.
(1) From a leadership perspective:

(2) From an individual contributor perspective:

Barriers to Inclusion Policies & Practices

ooo

The most common?

Common barriers to diversity and inclusion processes include but are not limited to:

(1) Poorly implemented diversity and inclusion strategies. Addressing change is an action that should inspire diversity of thought "<u>simultaneously</u>" throughout the organizational chart. In many instances, different levels of the organization are not aware of the extent of newly introduced initiatives;

(2) No accountability fostered at the mid-levels of leadership. Mid-level leaders tend to get stuck in a "non-

decision making mode" when deciding whether productivity is more important than the inclusion initiative itself. These leaders are consistently instructed to enhance diversity and inclusion mindsets throughout their workplace arena but not at the expense of the bottom line .... Or, it just always seems to happen that way;

(3) Diversity and inclusion related strategies are normally the last processes funded by an organization and are the first processes cut when budgets are questioned. This creates a constant start/stop delivery process that takes on a "flavor of the month" identity. Credibility is lost;

(4) Acts of systematic exclusion become another unexplainable result. Systematic exclusion occurs when no one in the organization can explain why there has been no positive movement toward a more respectful workplace and there is no one person who can be held directly accountable; And,

(5) Change strategies are introduced as a one-time training project instead of a consistently ingrained educational process for the total organization. There is no "magical dust" available to be sprinkled over an organization to make change automatically accepted. It is a long-term goal.

Are there other barriers to inclusion recognized in your workplace environment?

"BECAUSE IT'S THE RIGHT THING TO DO!"

o o o

Why is it hard to do the right thing?

A major theme of this book is to accept "common sense" as a given. Certain entities should do just that. Recognizing the need for a basic and true course of intervention may be all that's needed to bring about a basic, true result. As an example, common sense demands that if there are no women or people of color in decision-making positions in your organization, and deserving women and people of color are historically are passed over by "others" during promotional evaluations, etc., common sense then demands that the performance system needs to be challenged.

When obvious exclusion faces management, "Why can't they simply take the bull by the horns and do the right thing?" A six-month blue-ribbon commission is not needed to study this phenomenon before making strategic recommendations. If leadership is directly connected to honesty, decision-makers need very little time to push the effects of change policies. They merely must look in the mirror and just do what common sense dictates.

One's worldview or cultural lens may have something to do with this challenge. If decision makers never had to understand how other cultures think or feel, they may not have issues of inclusion on their radar screen. As they observed and emulated the leadership skills of those who preceded them, respecting cultural values may not have been taken into consideration for promotional reasons. Therefore, as they prepare for future upward mobility, they focus on other promotional aspects that are viewed as more important to the organization.

Why do you think it is so difficult "to do the right thing?"

BEHAVIORAL WASTE

ooo

What is it?

Behavioral waste comes in many forms. In a production context, the time it takes for the next assembly line employee to handle the same product is actually considered to be wasted seconds, or a form of behavioral waste.

When measuring the efficiency of human capital, behavioral waste occurs daily when employees give only a half-day's work for a whole day's pay because of a perceived lack of workplace respect. Behavioral waste also occurs when employees can't wait until the work day is over so they can "leave this place."

Behavioral waste occurs when employees "take as much sick time as possible" and find a reason "not to go to work." It occurs when employees sit idly at their desks thinking about how their supervisors really don't know the true value they bring to the workplace: Yet, can regularly produce an unworthy evaluation on an annual basis.

Where HR is involved, behavioral waste occurs whenever man-hours are spent responding to EEO complaints and discrimination lawsuits when their time can be used more productively in other ways.

The ABC's of Diversity:

Behavioral waste… whether intentional or non-intentional, has a negative affect on the organization's bottom-line. Positively addressing behavioral waste issues enhance workplace creativity, foster an environment of inclusion, and grow respect for the voices of other cultures… aspects that push for a more efficient organization.

(1) Identify other examples of behavioral waste in your workplace:

(2) Have you ever approached your organization with a recommendation that could enhance its level of efficiency? If not, why not? If so, how did management respond?

BIASES

o o o

Workplace Affect?

The workplace acknowledges many forms of bias. An intentional bias is one recognized and owned by an individual. However, it is still factored into the decision-making process along with its personal consequences.

The ABC's of Diversity:

Unintentional biases may be personal choices made with no understanding of how one's worldview or cultural lens affects a specific community. There can be no blame or finger pointing in this regard. We are all products of our ethnocentric experiences and none of us are similar. Our worldviews are formed from what we have experienced. We are who we are. However, the learning from our worldviews is one of ownership.

Once we have an opportunity to be more introspective, it is again a personal decision to learn more about ourselves. If we deny ourselves this opportunity, we would be denying ourselves the chance to become more cross-culturally competent. The organization will suffer from such a decision. We must first move ourselves before we can do so as a whole.

*Identify a personal bias you can discuss in an open forum.*_

———

BLAMING

o o o

Being the cause or source of something that occurred; to hold responsible; to find fault with; Blaming in a cultural context means that someone or a specific social segment must be held responsible because of a negative cultural attachment or association.

THE
BRUTAL
FACTS!

○ ○ ○

"How do you motivate people with brutal facts? Doesn't motivation flow chiefly from a compelling vision? Surprisingly, the answer is "No." Not because vision is unimportant, but because expending energy trying to motivate people is largely a waste of time. One of the dominant themes here is that you will not need to spend time and energy motivating your people. If you have the right people on the bus, they will be self-motivated. Then, the real question becomes: How do you manage in such a way as not to de-motivate people? And, one of the single most de-motivating actions you can take is to hold out false hopes, soon to be swept away by events.""...

"Yes, leadership is about vision. But leadership is equally about creating a climate where the truth is heard and the "brutal facts" confronted. There's a huge difference between the opportunity to "have your say" and the opportunity to be "heard." The good-to-great leaders understood this distinction, creating a culture wherein people had a tremendous opportunity to be heard and, ultimately, for the truth to be heard.""...

The ABC's of Diversity:

"How do you create a climate where the truth is heard? Here are four basic practices:
(1) Lead with questions, not answers? ...keep asking questions until you have a clear picture of reality and its implications. Use questions to gain an understanding and not as a form of manipulation;

(2) Engage in dialogue and debate, not coercion. All of the good-to-great companies partake in intense dialogue, with people engaged in a search for the best answers;

(3) Conduct autopsies, without blame. Take responsibility for bad decisions. When you conduct autopsies without blame, you go a long way toward creating a climate where truth is heard. If you have the right people on the bus, you should almost never need to assign blame but need only to search for understanding and learning; and,

(4) Build "red flag" mechanisms: A red flag is a non-transferable option to speak on any issue at any time in an effort to better any situation. There is no restriction on when and how to use your red flag; the decision rests entirely in your hands. You can use it to voice an observation, share a personal experience, present an analysis, disagree or challenge, ask a question, or whatever. The process will be stopped for your red flag. The key here is to use your red flag to turn useful information into "information that cannot be ignored" and for creating a climate where the truth (or, brutal facts) can be heard."
(6-Jim Collins, Good to Great, Chapter 4, pg 78, Harper Business Press, 2001)

The ABC's of Diversity:

(1) If you had the opportunity to discuss a "brutal fact" about your organization, what would it be?

(2) Would fear of retribution be a concern – either directly or indirectly?

"BUSINESS CASE" FOR DIVERSITY

o o o

"The dramatic rise in minority population and buying power has forced many corporations to rethink their long-term growth strategies and even the structure of their businesses. Unlike the affirmative action programs of the 1960's and 1970's, which were seen primarily as a way to redress the effects of past discrimination, the overriding incentive for the new wave of change is financial.

The ABC's of Diversity:

As American companies reach out to the markets of the new mainstream, they are being forced to reevaluate not only what they make and how they sell it, but also their internal values and human resource initiatives for recruitment, training, and employee motivation.

Corporations are learning that without a diverse workforce they will not only be at a disadvantage when it comes to hiring the best possible candidates, but they will also lack a cultural link to an increasingly critical part of their market. Thus, U.S. corporations are realizing that diversity in their workplace can help them: (1) increase profits and cut costs; (2) improve morale and boost productivity; (3) expand market share and develop new products and services; (4) cultivate new markets and position their brands for continued growth; and, (5) recruit and retain top talent."

7-(excerpt from The New Mainstream, Chapter 1, pg 21, written by Guy Garcia, Harper Collins Publisher, 2004)

CHANGING DEMOGRAPHICS

o o o

"America is a nation transformed by the fulfillment of its own ideas. Never has its population and culture been more vibrant and diverse, never has it been more reflective of – and connected to – the rest of the world. The new America is taking root in major cities, suburbs, and towns. The new America exists at the lowest rungs of the socioeconomic ladder and is striving for a better foothold at the top. The new America is defining – and defined by – the urban lifestyle, but it is also moving to the suburbs and smaller rural towns.

The new America is transforming life at the office, where managers seek to increase productivity by diversifying their workforce; at the beauty parlor, where Anglo socialites use hair relaxers created for African Americans; and on the internet, where online communities for Hispanics, Asians, African Americans, and other groups are competing with major portals for eyeballs and cyber-cash. It is changing how we look and what we drive, what we eat and why we eat it. Most of all, it is changing how people make money and spend it, where it comes from and where it is going.

The ABC's of Diversity:

Today, the 80 million Blacks, Hispanics, and Asians living in the United States make up more than one-fourth of the country and spend over $1.2 trillion a year.

By 2050, non-Anglos will have grown to47.2 percent of the population. Hispanics, Blacks, and Asians are already outpacing the rest of the United States in terms of population and income growth. The buying power of Latinos alone is growing at a compound rate of 8.7 percent - almost double that of non-Hispanics, and is projected to reach $926 billion by 2007. As a group, the nation's minorities purchase more consumer goods than the general population, are more brands loyal, and collectively represent other important new social patterns, influencing everything from images in advertising to attitudes about religion, family, education, and the afterlife.

The future is upon us, and the transformation of the mainstream has long since begun. To be sure, most Americans, to one degree or another, are aware that something important is happening. We know that if present demographic trends continue, European non-Hispanic whites will eventually be outnumbered, that Hispanics have overtaken African Americans as the country's largest minority, that foreign-born immigrants – both legal and undocumented – are changing the flavor, texture, and look of American neighborhoods, schools, and churches. We know that these newcomers are from many different countries, are of every race, and speak many languages, though often not English.

We might also know that salsa long ago replaced ketchup as the country's most popular condiment, that Oprah can make

Basic Words of Communication

or break a book, that gays have better taste than straights, and that women and people of color can and do run major corporations." *B*-(The New Mainstream: How the Multicultural Consumer is Transforming American Business, Introduction pg 10, written by Guy Garcia, Harper Collins Publishers, 2004)

CHEERLEADER,
COLLABORATOR,
&
CHALLENGER

o o o

Which are you?

There is a dire need for new and seasoned leaders to become "gutsier" by better understanding their cultural environment. Leaders need to acknowledge how their cultural worldviews factor into their personal leadership styles.

The book entitled "Gutsy Leadership: A Common Sense Workbook for Leadership Development, identifies Cheerleader, Collaborator, and Challenger as three gutsy leadership categories. The Cheerleader category is attached with leaders who support diversity initiatives "after" an organization's strategy has been announced. The Collaborator is a leader who supports the diversity initiative based on the level of employee/constituency buy-in. And,

The ABC's of Diversity:

the Challenger is one who is not afraid to independently challenge policies and procedures and one who constantly leads the charge for fresh, innovative thinking.

A further evaluation of each classification reveals that Challengers demonstrate gutsy leadership characteristics on a much more consistent basis. Collaborators and Cheerleaders - both acceptable levels of leadership - fit better into the "team player" category whereas a lesser level of personal risk taking in prevalent. Truly committed gutsy leaders, however, will probably not be "readily" found under the latter categories even though leadership can develop from within those classifications.

Challengers possess a "vision of a better, respectful, and more inclusive workplace that is simply too strong to resist." They have natural, proactive mindsets and are not afraid to act on their gut feelings.

(1) Which of these classifications best fits your leader(s) and why?

(2) Which best fits your leadership style?

Basic Words of Communication

CIRCLE
OF
INFLUENCE

o o o

"The 'Circle of Influence' refers to those things over which you "do" have control or influence such as: vision, discipline, passion and conscience.

Individual contributors who possess these elements are normally employees without significant positions or formal decision-making powers: yet, they can move themselves and their team or department in such a way that positively affects the entire organization."

9{(Stephen R. Covey's The 8th Habit: From Effectiveness to Greatness, chapter 7, pg 132, Free Press/Simon & Schuster)

Does your leadership recognize the value found within your "Circle of Influence?"

COACHING

o o o

"Coaching and mentoring have taken on a mystique. But, what's it all about? Is it for everyone? Does a good coach have to have more than a successful career to be drafted as the sounding board and cheerleader for a young star?

Coaching as a developmental strategy is not a "once and done." High potential leaders will need a succession of counselors, teachers, coaches and guides during the course of a successful career. Someone new to the organization may need an equally skilled peer in a similar job to show him or her how to overcome routine hurdles and get things done with a minimum of noise.

Research is beginning to show that minorities on a fast track need not only a good business coach but also opportunities to share their experiences with peers of racial and ethnic backgrounds. Ideally, formal one-to-one assignments are linked to other leadership development activities, business strategy, and human resource practice. Matching at the time of need is intentional and is best done outside of reporting hierarchy. Those identified as coaches agree to a specific time commitment; in some organizations this may be four to six hours a week. Designated coaches should be recommended for the role as a result of demonstrated success, not just personality traits and need to receive specialized training to ensure that coaching practice adheres to an institutional standard. Not all senior leaders are able to provide the motivation or feedback skill to serve as an effective coach.

Again, coaching is an ongoing development strategy. Its focus grows from orientation to the business and task at the beginning of a relationship to feedback and counseling around behavioral practice that binds self-awareness."
10-(Talent Management Handbook, Lance Berger and Dorothy Berger, Chapter 27, pg 297, Integrating Coaching, Training, and Development with Talent Management (Helen Krewson), McGraw Hill Publishers, 2004)

CORPORATE CULTURE

o o o

How to Recognize an Inclusive Culture?

"American culture, diverse subcultures, and corporate culture each play important roles in the ability of your company to hire and retain the diverse talent it needs, because people must fit it if they are to stay and contribute. You and each employee play an important role in making your corporate culture the type that welcomes people from diverse backgrounds and includes them in the "inner circle." Your ability to build profitable workplace relationships with these people may determine your job success. Does your organization have the following qualities? (1) A two-way company-employee cultural adaptation process that is really a cultural orientation process that occurs when new employees join the organization. Through this process they learn not only about company procedures and employee benefits, but also the organization's culture – its values, do's and don'ts, legends, champions, and rituals – the way we do things around here. They values and norms may be more difficult for diverse employees to learn because they are usually not part of the Euro-American cliques and grapevines;

(2) Interdependence; or, "How interdependent are people in your corporate culture? The evolution from independence to interdependence is reflected in the American business culture generally and in the corporate cultures of leading organizations. Just as the culture at large ties people together and gives meaning and purpose to their everyday lives, corporate culture is the glue that holds corporations together;

(3) Is your organization strong and participative? The stronger and more participative the corporate culture, the more success it is likely to experience in shifting toward inclusion. In weak corporate cultures, leaders do not clearly communicate a set of core values that are reinforced by role models, myths, rituals, and symbols. Employees naturally stick with their own culture group's norms and values. Employee's have more freedom to determine how to act, but if the culture is too weak, they go off in all directions and have great difficulty coordinating their work with others.

In strong corporate cultures, leaders clearly define and enforce values and norms, giving more direction to how people should act, more reinforcement about what they should do, and perhaps higher penalties for not conforming. Strong participative cultures are more democratic. Leaders clearly communicate a few core values that define their mission – why a company is in business and what makes it successful. They require all employees to buy into these values and to observe them in their decisions and actions;

(4) Flexible in adapting to a diversity of employee needs and talents. Employees who come to the organization with quite different viewpoints, values, needs, and work approaches are most likely to feel valued and to succeed in a corporate culture that's flexible enough to provide a welcoming niche for them. To increase flexibility, corporations are: Customizing mentoring programs; Making job assignments that ensure a progression of sympathetic and supportive supervisors; Assigning newcomers to a series of problem-solving task forces so they can form a series of peer relationships that sustain them through the early years; Developing explicit guidelines for all employees about working with minorities and a procedure for making everyone aware of these guidelines; Specifying standards for social behavior in relationships minorities; and, Removing ritualistic cultural barriers to the acceptance of minorities;

(5) Tolerant of reasonable nonconformity. Just how comfortable do people generally feel about differences, uncertainty, debate, and other forms of nonconformity? In inclusive cultures, these are all viewed as normal and potentially useful rather than as dysfunctional and threatening; and,

(6) Appreciative of the contributions diverse employees make to organization success and profitability." Companies that are creating inclusive corporate cultures recognize and experience a surprising wealth of benefits at all levels – personal, interpersonal, and organizational."

The ABC's of Diversity:

Some of these benefits are: Increasing personal skills for relating to customers, suppliers, and others in a global marketplace; Attracting and retaining the best available human talent; Creating and innovating from a more powerful diverse pool of talent; and, Contributing to social responsibility by providing success opportunities for people from all groups. //- (taken from Diversity Success Strategies, Chapter 2, pg 46, written by Norma-Carr Ruffino, Butterworth/Heinemann Publishers, 1999)

How would you describe your corporate culture?

CORPORATE SUCCESSION PLANNING

o o o

"In today's competitive environment, diversity is a key element to a successful succession planning process. When properly acknowledged, diversity provides realistic and achievable goals that are competitively advantageous and beneficial to both the individual and the organization. Diversity, integrated within the succession planning process, forms the strategic alliance between management and the

The ABC's of Diversity:

diverse workforce to ensure the retention and development of future leaders who represent a variety of backgrounds.

Succession planning strategies must recognize each employee regardless of race, color, religion, gender, or disability as a valued individual contributor, promote the existence of a fair system of workplace equality, and reflect a diversity philosophy whose intent is easily understood by its employees. It is then easier for the best and brightest to commit tot eh company for the long term, knowing that their commitment to the company is shared by the company's commitment to them.

Succession planning approaches that incorporate diversity strategies add a significant level of complexity to a process that may be very vague. The more clearly delineated the succession process, the easier it will be to create a more diverse workforce. Diversity-focused Succession planning Risks include: the perception that the leadership development process for key performers is highly subjective and full of favoritism vs. a more objective approach; executive sabotage because of the perception that it only helps minorities advance; the organization's climate could easily act as a barrier to any succession planning process; corporate leaders my feel as though minority members will not ever adopt culturally to the company's values; and, the organization could be "unconsciously" resistant to upsetting the status quo."

Six reasons to include diversity in the succession plan are:
(1) It encourages and enables all employees to draw fully on their talents and skills for the benefit of the business;

Basic Words of Communication

The ABC's of Diversity:

(2) A competitive advantage will come to those companies that best adapt to incorporating diverse groups into their leadership development environment;

(3) It better reflects the customer/client mix;

(4) It enhances organizational decision-making by offering alternative opinions and perspectives;

(5) It shows the public that the company is fair in its practices; and,

(6) It minimizes disillusionment in diverse groups, ensuring greater participation in business procedures and practices.

A successful diversity-focused succession planning process will contribute to a strong, integrated culture that reinforces an organization's vision, strategy, and goals. A creative diversity-based succession planning process attracts and keeps the most talented employees, provides outstanding returns to shareholders and stakeholders, and has a guiding purpose that inspires loyalty and long-term commitment to the organization."

12-(Building a Reservoir of High Potential Women and Diverse Groups, Leon T Lanier, Sr., The Talent Management Handbook by Berger and Berger, Chapter 10, page 273, Mcgraw-Hill, 2004.)

Describe the succession planning process, official or unofficial, as you see it in your organization.

CREATING
THE
"MEDICI"
EFFECT

o o o

What is the Medici Effect?

The idea behind The Medici Effect is a simple one that concerns itself with how cultures can interact and benefit from each other. "When you step into an intersection of fields, disciplines, or cultures, you can combine existing concepts into a large number of extraordinary new ideas. The name given to this phenomenon, the Medici Effect, comes from a remarkable burst of creativity in fifteenth-century Italy. The Medicis were a banking family in Florence who funded creators from a wide range of disciplines. Thanks to this family and a few others like it, sculptors, scientists, poets, philosophers, financiers, painters, and architects converged upon the city of Florence. There they found each other, learned from one another, and broke down the barriers between disciplines and cultures. Together they forged a new world based on new ideas – what became known as the Renaissance Era. As a result, the city became the epicenter of a creative explosion, one of the most innovative eras in history.

The Medici family can be felt even to this day. We, too, can create the Medici Effect. We can ignite this explosion of extraordinary ideas and take advantage of it as individuals, as teams, and as organizations. We can do so by bringing together different disciplines and cultures and searching for the places they connect. In retrospect, the Medici Effect is not about that specific era but about "those elements that made that era possible." It is about what happens when you step into an intersection of different cultures. And bring the ideas you find there to life." - Similar to culturally-related strategies we strive to design and implement in this present era! *13*(Excerpts from "The Medici Effect: Breakthrough Insights at the Intersection of Ideas, Concepts, and Cultures. Frans Johansson, Introduction pg 2, Harvard Business School Press, 2004.)

What is your perspective concerning the Medici Theory?

CROSS-
CULTURAL
COMPETENCE

°°°

What is cross-cultural competence?

Many definitions exist and each is just as valuable as the other. I define cross-cultural competence as "a skill level of introspective readiness where individual contributors can honestly identify cultural biases of their own and of others and still respectfully honor the worldviews and cultural lens found across the wide diversity spectrum."

Being cross-culturally competent affords you the ability to: (1) identify and understand your own and another's world views for the sake of better interpreting cultural related scenarios; (2) make better personal decisions on how to develop an acceptable mindset in that regard; and, (3) resolve situations in ways that optimize personal learning of cultural differences.

The business case for taking cross-cultural competency to a higher level is that it directly affects productivity which in turn affects the company's bottom-line. Behavioral waste is just one of those areas affected. How much of an employee's production time is wasted discussing issues of non-inclusion? How productive can an employee actually be when workplace respect has to be recaptured on a daily basis? Why should employees give 100 percent when they are not valued as highly as those who look different than

The ABC's of Diversity:

they? If you can imagine a workplace where such questions are being asked, then you can probably imagine the tremendous amount of wasted production time. Employees need and want to bring their best self to a workplace that is free from cultural biases and negative stereotypes. Developing a higher level of cross-cultural competence allows these issues to be discovered and discussed to enhance a more respectful, productive workplace. It is definitely worth the investment in human capital.

Cross-cultural competence is also a measure of how well worldviews of individuals from other countries and nations are understood and accepted in America. To enhance cross-cultural competence skills organizationally and individually, we must remain open to all aspects of diversity. An article written for Profiles and Diversity Journal (July 2005) listed ten (10) important ways to measure your organization's level of cross-culturally competence.

Your organization is cross-culturally competent if you can:
(1) Acknowledge that cultural biases will always exist – agreeing that society is not a perfect state;

(2) Learn more about and explore other cultures if only to validate personal and organizational culture biases;

(3) Realize that diversity is broader than just racial, religious, and color issues and includes the disabled, elderly, and uneducated, etc.;

(4) Understand that globally the world is a smaller place and, therefore, imperative to better understand other cultures;

Basic Words of Communication

The ABC's of Diversity:

(5) Accept that the face of America, the world, is constantly changing and the diversity spectrum will definitely expand;

(6) Ingrain cross-cultural competence as an educational process throughout the organization – not as a one time training event;

(7) Integrate all cultures for the benefit of a respectful work environment;

(8) Understand the connection between the level of cross-cultural competence and the bottom-line;

(9) Accept constructive cultural feedback without adopting a defensive attitude; and,

(10) Encourage freedom of expression and opinions without fear of reprisals or retribution.

(1) On a scale of 1 to 10, where would you rate your level of cross-cultural competence? Explain why?

(2) On the same scale, where would you rate the level of cross-cultural competence observed in your specific workplace environment? Explain.

Basic Words of Communication

The ABC's of Diversity:

Lanier Diversity Consultants'

CROSS-CULTURAL COMPETENCE SELF-ASSESSMENT INSTRUMENT

(Confidential)

o o o

The following workplace issues involve some dimension of cross-cultural competence. Please read each and assign a value of 1 – 10 based on how closely each represents your mindset. If an issue is one you've never experienced, select a value based on your initial reaction.

(1 = totally disagree vs. 10 = totally agree).

The ABC's of Diversity:

Confidential Cross-Cultural Competence Self-Assessment:

(1) I can look at newly hired Asians and other ethnicities and see them only as valued coworkers – not as a different cultural group. _____

(2) Leaders are reluctant to acknowledge their "inexperience" in cross-cultural issues for fear of having their leadership capabilities challenged. _____

(3) If "people of color" are smart, loyal, and hard working employees, upward mobility will be a natural progression. _____

(4) Employees with different worldviews must change them and make them conform to corporate policies. _____

(5) There tends to be a different level of personal scrutiny whenever candidates from "other cultures" are interviewed for a higher job classification. _____

(6) When I hear other cultures referred to as "you people," I don't think the term is a "non-exclusive" one. _____

(7) There's nothing unethical about employees being evaluated as "not ready", then given the responsibility of training the next promoted supervisor. _____

Basic Words of Communication

The ABC's of Diversity:

(8) If certain cultural segments of our society are apprehensive about challenging the status quo, it's probably their fault that the status quo never changes._____

(9) Its easier for whites to evaluate other cultures than for other cultures to evaluate whites.   _____

(10) Its very hard to locate, recruit and retain the "best and most talented" members of other cultures.   _____

(11) A person hired because of an organization's "quota" policy needs more time to learn the system.   _____

(12) Great leaders alter their leadership styles based on the specific culture to be led.   _____

(13) Because a policy is a top-down corporate mandate, it should naturally cross all cultural boundaries.

          _____

(14) When mid-level leaders have to choose between "doing the right thing" versus "meeting production numbers", meeting production tends to be the choice.   _____

(15) I understand other cultures because several of my best friends are people from other cultures.   _____

(16) When I am in a meeting attended by many ethnicities, I feel uncomfortable sharing my experiences.   _____

Basic Words of Communication

The ABC's of Diversity:

(17) When I have a conversation with my Hispanic boss, I find it difficult to make direct eye contact. _____

(18) The key to a higher evaluation is not based on work ethic, but more on one's ability to "fit in" with the current cultural status quo. _____

(19) The term "That's the way things are around here!" generally relates to policy and not culture. _____

(20) As a proven leader of my organization's dominant class, I have the natural ability to provide open and honest feedback to those I supervise, regardless of cultural affiliation. _____

(21) My understanding of other cultures is based on my ability to get along with everybody and by treating everyone the same. _____

(22) Workplace respect is a common experience for all cultures in my organization. _____

(23) My organization proactively seeks inclusion in any way possible. _____

(24) The elderly and disabled deal with less workplace exclusion than those who are culturally different.

_____

Basic Words of Communication

The ABC's of Diversity:

(25) African Americans are more culturally sensitive today because of their relationship to past oppressions.

_____

(26) White females and "females of color" probably have very similar worldviews.   _____

(27) When I enter the workplace, I alter my personality to one more accepting of cultural differences.   _____

(28) I am culturally sensitive in both the workplace and my private social setting.   _____

(29) African Americans would rather seek the truth about an issue versus simply making peace to settle it.

_____

(30) African Americans feel they have to be twice as good to obtain the same workplace value as whites.   _____

(31) White men have more of a sense of entitlement when it comes to their roles in this society.   _____

(32) Asian Americans are stereotyped as having inherited tremendous academic skills.   _____

(33) I can dismiss sexual orientation as someone else's issue that actually doesn't affect me.   _____

Basic Words of Communication

The ABC's of Diversity:

(34) Gay, Lesbian, Transgender and Bi-sexual communities are perceived as different cultures. _____

(35) Leaders who have successfully supervised ethnicities in this country are very capable of leading in a different global climate. _____

(36) When classes of people are consistently denied upward mobility, it still doesn't mean there's a direct link to management's lack of accountability. _____

(37) Although cultural insensitivity may be present, awareness of such insensitivities may not be to the owner. _____

(38) I go out of my way to learn more about other cultures. _____

(39) English should be the first language of this nation. _____

(40) This nation, as a whole, is actually very accepting of other cultures. _____

(41) To not be cross-culturally competent means you "intentionally" made past decisions that were probably insensitive to another's worldview. _____

Basic Words of Communication

The ABC's of Diversity:

(42) I would challenge my organization's workplace policies regardless of possible retribution. _____

(43) To become more cross-culturally competent, you must better understand other cultures as well as your own.

_____

(44) I see very few "others" at the executive level. This will automatically change as our customer base changes.

_____

(45) Cultural differences have not affected any of my personnel decisions at the workplace. _____

(46) I work in an environment where I can learn about differences and practice those learnings. _____

(47) Cultural differences are perceived differently in other countries. _____

(48) While learning to better understand other cultures, it is okay to do so at your own pace. _____

(49) Acknowledging another's culture does not mean you have to "accept" that culture as your own, only "respect" it as theirs. _____

Basic Words of Communication

The ABC's of Diversity:

(50) The Golden Rule is not "to treat others as you would have them treat you", but instead, "to treat others as they wish to be treated."   _____

For results and analysis please visit our website @ LanierDiversityConsultants.com and follow the instructions for your personal and confidential scale.

Cultural Audit

o o o

Audit of an organization's culture and quality of work life in an organization; Measuring the gap between the employee's perceived culture and the culture which is reality.

Cultural Business Differences

o o o

Cultural differences can and will directly affect how well we interact in the global business world. In many instances, the business mindset of other countries is not similar to that of the western world. As an example, in several countries in South America, just because an agreement on a contract has been made does not mean the process will move forward at that time. This time lapse can be interpreted as behavioral waste by one business culture but a business necessity by the other - as that culture uses more time to observe potential partners.

Policy-making for multi-national corporations tends to come from the United States and passed on to companies located across the world. Understanding how other cultures do business is key to being successful.

Does your organization offer a learning process that explains the cultural mindsets of current and/or future global partners? If so, describe this learning process.

CULTURAL LENS

o o o

Cultural lens are worldviews that allow you to evaluate culturally sensitive issues through observation and/or interaction. Your ethnocentric experiences developed your sensitivity to culture related issues. This combination of maturities help you interpret how to respond to culture-related situations lived out each day.

The ABC's of Diversity:

The following is an example of a cultural lens. It is one that includes personal ownership, placing blame and judging the ethnocentric experiences of others, and developing a personal path-forward strategy for future mindset development.

I graduated from Chester, Pennsylvania's Middle and High Schools during the 1960's. I was completely naïve about cultural exclusion at that time. Thus, I never challenged the School Board's lack of a Black History curriculum. Through this accepted ignorance, I developed a worldview or cultural lens that was probably not as accurate as a proud Honor Student's should be. I thought this educational "omission" was an intentional decision by the completely white School Board to neither respect nor develop the mindsets of people of color.

As I matured as an adult, I carried an opinion that white people were so entitled, they really didn't want the truth told – whatever those truths were, and that discrimination of thought was the way of the western world. My cultural development told me... "that's just the way things were" back in those days.

As I experience today's corporate world as a diversity practitioner, I give tremendous thought to why it's hard sometimes for white people to ... "Get it?" Everything from entitlement to birthright comes to mind but I think I have another personal issue that reeks of exclusion. If I accepted my theory as factual, then decisions made in the

Basic Words of Communication

The ABC's of Diversity:

1960's by the School Administration may have negatively affected white students just as much as it did students of color. I never gave such a possibility any thought. My worldview from that moment on has been an "exclusive" one to say the least.

Some thirty years later, this nation is seeking a respectful workplace and wondering why it's difficult for all of America's mindsets to comply. When, in retrospect, thirty long years of cultural development and ethnocentric experiences by white students could have readily created barriers that prevent them from "getting it!" Hence, my worldview on this issue has significantly changed.

This is just one example of how I've re-evaluated a cultural experience of yesteryear to better understand one of my current worldviews. Ownership is a critical part of learning.

(1) Think of a situation that occurred during your early years that may have affected the development of your cultural lens. Describe how it affects you now.

Basic Words of Communication

"Culturally, It's okay to be where you are" But,

○ ○ ○

No one has experienced life as you know it. You were
created differently. No one has walked in your shoes. No
one has felt your feelings of joy or your pains of sorrow… as
only "you" processed it. Even those closely related to you
may not understand the real you. They only know the
personal side of you that you allowed them to see in your
everyday actions. You've interpreted the beliefs and values
passed down by your parents and decided which to keep and
which you will not. Your brother and/or sister, raised in the
same household, still developed different personalities by
adulthood even thought they went through many of the same
experiences.

No one processed your ethnocentric experiences as you
processed them. Your thoughts at an early age created a

The ABC's of Diversity:

decision-making foundation for choices you still make today. As you grew in age, so did your ability to interpret who you wanted to be.

Your ability to interpret the mindset of your neighborhoods, churches, schools, and segments of society that looked just like you established acceptable norms of who you are and the best way for you to survive in this world.

Now, as an adult, you have learned that the American culture hasn't exactly been an inclusive one. Strangers who don't reside in your neighborhood are asking you to change in the best interest of the corporation. There has been no blaming. There has been no finger-pointing on entitlement issues at the workplace. No one has accused you of anything or asked you to do anything other than become more aware of inclusion policies and practices. No one is forcing you to do anything you don't want to do. The cultural world is only asking you join it as an open-minded, inclusive member.

This country was born under a "freedom of choice" theme based on different philosophies grown across a giant ocean. Globally, now that the ocean is smaller, the choice is again... yours! Even though you are where you are cross-culturally competent-wise, when it comes to increasing your level of respect and sensitivity, the greater value of society seeks your support!

Is there a noticeable cultural gap in your organization?

Basic Words of Communication

CULTURE

ooo

Exactly what is Culture?

The Encyclopedia Britannica describes "culture" as the integrated pattern of human knowledge, belief, and behavior.... Language, ideas, beliefs, customs, taboos, codes, institutions, techniques, rituals, and other related components...."

Another way of defining culture is by understanding its connection with "values." Values are those things (beliefs) you hold so dearly to your heart and those things that mold your decision-making processes. *Culture, therefore, is how you live out those values and beliefs within a given community.*

"Culture is the environment you live in. You learned it from your parents, teachers, the media, everyone and everything you knew as you grew up. Culture is what a particular group agrees is reality. It becomes the backdrop for the way people think, feel, speak and act. For every aspect of culture that we're aware of, there are about 1,000 aspects that we're unaware of. Culture is far more than mere custom that can be easily changed from the outside, even though it's always changing and evolving naturally from the inside. Surface aspects may change rapidly, but core aspects tend to be very resistant to change."

14 (taken from Diversity Success Strategies, Chapter 2, pg 18, written by Norma-Carr Ruffino, Butterworth/Heinemann Publishers, 1999)

CULTURE
CHANGE
IS
INEVITABLE!

o o o

Or, is it?

Remember those early days when you first started school? The first thing you may have noticed was that each child was different. It was important that you learned how to be a part of that classroom's cultural environment even though your worldview or cultural lens experience thus far was minimal. You were so anxious to address life's transition. Accepting and developing a mindset for change was inevitable and there was nothing you wanted to do about it.

Let's talk about those early adolescent years. Impressionable children turning into teenagers... Learning more and more from ethnocentric experiences and adopting future maturation mindsets. Then, witnessing personal growth to young adulthood. Change, again, was inevitable. Although questioning your responsibility to the world, there was nothing you wanted to do to stop life's progress. Freedom of choice was developing within and you eagerly learned how to use it.

The ABC's of Diversity:

Alas, adulthood. An identity has been acknowledged. You are now who you are. Your cultural identity has emerged with whatever biases attached. Your schools, homes, neighborhoods, colleges, and peer groups taught you how to decide between right from wrong and how to survive this world.

America's workplace is changing faster than yesteryear's Industrial Revolution – figuratively and culturally. You've awakened one morning and found that your workplace initiative has changed to one that seeks respect, inclusiveness, and equality for all. You are asked to become more open-minded concerning diversity issues... a thought that never crossed your mind yesterday. Freedom of choice is abundant. The ability to change has now taken on an added burden. A major question for you to now ask yourself? *"Have I culturally reached a point of no return?"*

(1) Have you culturally reached a point of no return? A point in your life where understanding and respecting the cultures of others is not high on your list of priorities?

(2) What would it take to renew or enhance your interest?

Basic Words of Communication

The ABC's of Diversity:

○ ○ ○

Defense, in a cultural worldview context as described by the Intercultural Development Inventory (IDI), "indicates that you have a strong commitment to your own worldview and some distrust of cultural behavior or ideas that differ from your own. You are aware of other cultures around you, but you may have a relatively incomplete understanding of them and you probably have fairly strong negative stereotypes about some of them. As an example, if you have a good relationship with a coworker, neighbor, or friend from another culture, you may consider that person an exception to the rule about the group to which he or she belongs."

15-(Excerpt from the Intercultural Development Inventory Manual by Dr. Mitch Hammer and Dr. Milton Bennett, 1998).

(1) Do you think your particular culture is better than other cultures found in the US? Why or why not?

(2) Do you think your culture is better than those found throughout the world? Why or why not?

Basic Words of Communication

DENIAL

○○○

Denial, as described in a cultural worldview context by the Intercultural Development Inventory (IDI), is basically described as "an ego defense mechanism that operates either consciously or unconsciously to resolve emotional conflict by refusing to perceive the more unpleasant aspects of external reality. Culturally speaking, denial may be an indication that you are more comfortable with the familiar and are not anxious to complicate life with cultural difference (i.e., you may simply not notice much cultural difference around you.)"

"One example of cultural denial is that you may be unaware of a minority population in your area or you may be disinterested in multicultural or international affairs that do not immediately affect you. Another example may be when you maintain separation from others who are different (i.e., selection neighborhoods were neighborhoods are culturally similar to you)."

16-(taken from the Intercultural Development Inventory Manual by Dr. Mitch Hammer and Dr. Milton Bennett, 1998).

Is it possible to be in denial and actually not know it? Discuss your opinion in a learning forum.

The ABC's of Diversity:

Dialogue
vs.
Debate

○ ○ ○

How does each differ?

There is quite a difference between having good dialogue and having good communication. The difference is that dialogue is communication at its highest level. There are so many different ways to communicate (i.e. verbal, facial, attitude, posture). Yet, the measure of understanding is generated by how well each voice understands what the other is saying... without having what, in reality, is an unwanted debate.

The Six Basic Rules of Dialogue are as follows: (1) Be open and suspend judgments; (2) Keep dialogue and decision-making separate because dialogue precedes decision-making, negotiation or action; (3) Speak for yourself and treat all participants as peers; (4) Listen with empathy; (5) Look for common ground – identifying areas where you agree; and, (6) Search for and disclose hidden assumptions – especially in yourself.

A good dialogue also offers certain benefits. It dispels mistrust; breaks through negative stereotypes; shifts from the impersonal to the creation of community; makes participants more sympathetic to one another even when they disagree; prepares groundwork for decision-making although no decisions are made at this time; helps to bridge subcultures;

Basic Words of Communication

The ABC's of Diversity:

expands the number of people committed to the process; brings out the best in people; and, creates a climate of good faith.

Debate, on the other hand, assumes that there is one right answer (and, you have it). A debate is an attempt to prove that the other perspectives are wrong and it is all about winning. Debate is about listening for flaws that open the door for counter-arguments. It is about defending your assumptions and criticizing the other side's point of view. Debate also occurs when you seek an outcome that agrees with your position.

Every time I revisit this list, I paused to do some introspection. Was my last attempt at dialogue really that or was it a poor process of communication? Or, maybe somewhere in the middle?

I now realize I had not done a great job of it. Again, a lesson to be learned.

(1) Evaluate your communication skills level.

(2) Evaluate the skill levels observed within your organization.

70
Basic Words of Communication

DISABILITIES:
MYTHS
&
REALITIES

o o o

"People usually don't openly express their attitudes of avoidance or discomfort toward persons with disabilities. For example, most people don't voice their pity or distaste, nor avoid all eye contact, conversation, touching, or proximity. Avoidance attitudes are more likely to be expressed indirectly in the form of exclusionary practices, sometimes said to be necessary for the safety or convenience of persons with disabilities, or of people in general. The result is that most people don't have persons with disabilities around them, which relieves them from being uncomfortable or distressed."

"Myth number one: persons with disabilities are childlike, dependent, and in need of charity or pity; (2) disabled people are unable to lead normal lives; (3) they can only do menial jobs and most don't like to work; (4) they create safety risks and are less productive than other workers; and (5), are more difficult to work with. Persons with disabilities are consistently devalued in the eyes of others."
/7-(Norma-Carr Ruffino, Diversity Success Strategies, Chapter 10, pg 240, Butterworth/Hieneman, 1999)

The ABC's of Diversity:

Are there any issues about the disabled you would like to discuss in an open "learning" forum? Issues or thoughts that may help clarify biases grown by your ethnocentric experiences?

DISCRIMINATION

o o o

Prejudice or differentiation in the screening, hiring, promoting, discharging, of individuals based on race, religion, place of birth, or other non-job-related reasons. "You can discriminate by merely being part of an organization that unintentionally discriminates through its traditional business practices. This is because of the "power-privilege imbalance" that automatically favors a dominant majority and disfavors minorities – unless actions are taken to offset the imbalance.

A power imbalance is a key aspect of discrimination because power is a force that is absolutely essential to perpetuate discrimination. For example, an African American female clerk may dislike a Euro-American executive and never try to get to know him as a person. Her actions are not called

Basic Words of Communication

discrimination because she does not have the power to take actions that exclude him in ways that disadvantage his career. Likewise, a "<u>privilege imbalance</u>" goes hand in hand with a power imbalance, meaning there is a powerful group with distinct privileges that other groups don't have."
18-(Norma-Carr Ruffino, Diversity Success Strategies, Chapter 2, pg 65, Butterworth/Heinemann Press, 1999)

DISCUSSING
THE
"UNDISCUSSABLES"[99]

○○○
What are Undiscussables?

"Undiscussables" are taboo workplace concerns many employees refuse to openly talk about because of personal and/or organizational restrictions (perceived or not) and from the fear of being negatively labeled by management. Workplace respect and equality issues like race and gender quickly come to mind as several topics hard to discuss in a workplace community.

An open forum is critical to any path-forward diversity strategy. A safe environment for freedom of expression must be created if leaders really want to hear "how things really are around here," Until this safe speaking environment is established, the direction of the company will not travel on the right journey. "One of the most powerful

The ABC's of Diversity:

ways to begin overcoming workplace fear is to discuss the workplace's undiscussables. It is a rich technique for accessing the hidden issues and problems covered up in relationships, work groups, and the organization as a whole. Discussing the undiscussables is not a one time event. It can be an excellent approach for a team-building retreat or special problem-solving meeting. It is also a principle of disclosure that should become a part of everyday communication. Several strategies / results are as follows:

(1)   Introduce the concept so that others will understand the dynamics of issues that are hard to bring up;

(2)   Describe the process and set the ground rules;

(3)   Identify the undiscussables so that participants will know what others have a hard time talking about;

(4)   Talk about the undiscussable issues for shared clarity and understanding; and,

(5)   Follow through to ensure action on issues that need to be and can be addressed.

Work with core undiscussables so that participants leave the discussion with an understanding of the emotions at the heart of their reluctance to speak up."3.
19 (Kathleen Ryan & Daniel Ostreich; Driving Fear out of the Workplace: Creating a High Trust High Performance Organization; Second Edition, pg 209; Chapter 12, Discuss the Undiscussables; Jossey-Bass, 1998.) pg 64;

Basic Words of Communication

The ABC's of Diversity:

List other undiscussables you would like to discuss in an open forum.

DIVERSITY...

Diversity can be described as a state of being, a mindset of cultural acceptance, and a path forward organizational reality that enhances corporate bottom-lines.

Diversity is also the collective mixture of differences and similarities in the workforce. This include things such as race, gender, thinking styles, culture, sexual orientation, age, nationality and religion, to name a few.

What is your definition of diversity?

Has it changed over the years?

The ABC's of Diversity:

"DRIVING HUMAN CAPITAL"

o o o

How many times have organizations looked outside of its current employee base to fill a specific position? When this occurs, two negative perceptions may develop. One negative perception may be the organizational value attached to its own human capital recognition system. The other may question the organization's personnel development process. Both, however, affect career mindsets of those associated with its talent pool.

"Driving human capital," in a cultural equity context, recommends that decision-makers look more internally for answers to their promotional needs. Many times, when those classified as "most ready" are women and/or minorities, a process of "systematic exclusion" tends to manifest a more biased advancement practice. Suddenly, names topping the talent pool require a more scrutinized process. When this happens, it represents nothing short of a biased double standard and creates natural barriers to corporate inclusion policies.

The theory is to establish a diverse talent pool of candidates and, after properly developing them for leadership, trust them by creating a support system for success. By doing so,

The ABC's of Diversity:

it shows respect for your current talent and enhances the diversity vision of the corporation's future.

The workplace needs motivators. Respect for any upward mobility function is a valid example of one. Employees will be more productive in work climates where upward mobility is not only respected but a built-in career factor. A possible metric is to consider how often you seek external talent.

How effectively does your workplace develop its human capital potential?

EFFECTIVE
COMMUNICATION

o o o

Effective communication occurs when the intended meaning of the "deliverer" of the information and the perceived meaning of the "listener" are one and the same.

Are effective communication skills apparent in your workplace? Why or why not?

EMERGING TALENT

o o o

Emerging talent is a term applied to those employees who are within five to ten years of college who have shown extraordinary vision and leadership ability. They are often supported, coached, and tracked until they reach the high potential pool of talent.

EMPLOYEE EMPOWERMENT

o o o

Employee empowerment occurs when you grant employees power to initiate change, thereby encouraging them to take charge of what they do.

EMPLOYEE INVOLVEMENT

o o o

Employee Involvement is a participative process that uses the entire capacity of employees and is designed to encourage increased commitment to the organization's success.

ETHICAL DECISIONS

o o o

The Corporate World Reality?

Personal beliefs are about what is right and what is wrong or good or bad. "Making ethical decisions is easy when facts are clear and the choices are black and white. But it is a different story when the situation is clouded by ambiguity, incomplete information, multiple points of view, and conflicting responsibilities. In such situations – which managers experience all the time – ethical decisions depend on both the decision-making process itself and on the experience, intelligence, and integrity of the decision-maker. Responsible moral judgment cannot be transferred to decision makers ready-made. Developing it in business turns out to be partly an administrative process involving: recognition of a decision's ethical implications; discussion to expose different points of view; and, testing the tentative decision's adequacy in balancing self-interest and consideration of others, its import for future policy, and its consonance with the company's traditional values.

Ethical decisions therefore require of individuals three qualities that can be identified and developed. (1) The first is competence to recognize ethical issues and to think through the consequences of alternative resolutions; (2) The second is self-confidence to seek out different points of view and then to decide what is right at a given time or place, in a particular set of relationships and circumstances. And (3), the willingness to make decisions when all that needs to be known cannot be known and when the questions that press for answers have no established and incontrovertible solutions."4.

20-(The Harvard Business Review on Corporate Ethics. Ethics in Practice by Kenneth R. Andrews, pg 71-72, Harvard Business School Press, 2003) pg 72;

On a scale of 1-10, how ethical would you rate your organization? If your response is a 7 or lower, please offer an explanation.

ETHNICITY

o o o

Members of ethnic and so-called "racial" groups commonly use ethnic symbols as badges of identity to emphasize their distinctness from other groups. Language, religion, and style of dress are common ethnic symbols. In addition to such cultural traits, biological characteristics may be important at times as well. Ethnic group unity needs to be reinforced by a constant emphasis on what traits set the members apart from others, rather than what they share in common with the outsiders.

ETHNIC PREJUDICE

o o o

"People who try to distinguish between race and ethnicity typically say that racial traits are inborn, inherited, and given by nature, while ethnic traits are learned, cultural, and acquired through nurture. Since most of the characteristics that vary from culture to culture are learned and are not permanently fixed in our genes, they can theoretically be changed. Ethnicity is much more flexible and changeable than race.

The ABC's of Diversity:

An ethnic subculture is a segment of a larger culture of society. Members of the subculture participate in shared activities in which the common origin and culture are significant ingredients. A subculture is unique because of its particular beliefs, values, and customs, its heroes and heroines, its myths and stories, and its social networks. Ethnic discrimination against minority subcultures occurs when minority status carries with it the exclusion from full participation in the society and the largest subculture holds an undue share of power, influence, and wealth in society."

21-(taken from Diversity Success Strategies, Chapter 3, pg 67, written by Norma-Carr Ruffino, Butterworth/Heinemann Publishers, 1999) pg 73;

ETHNOCENTRIC
&
ETHORELATIVE
STAGES

o o o

"The Intercultural Development Inventory (IDI) developed by Dr. Mitchell Hammer and Dr. Milton Bennett measures intercultural sensitivity as conceptualized in Bennett's Developmental Model of Intercultural Sensitivity (DMIS).

The DMIS is a framework for explaining the reactions of people to cultural differences. The underlying assumption of

The ABC's of Diversity:

the model is that as one's experience of cultural differences becomes more complex, one's potential competence in intercultural interactions increases. Dr. Bennett has identified a set of fundamental cognitive structures (or worldviews) that act as orientations to cultural difference. The worldviews vary from the more ethnocentric (One's own culture is viewed as central to one's reality) to the more ethnorelative (One's own culture is experienced in the context of "other" cultures). According to the DMIS theory, more ethnorelative worldviews have more potential to generate the attitudes, knowledge, and behavior that constitute intercultural competence.

The IDI measures an individual's (or groups) fundamental worldview orientation to cultural difference, and thus the individual's or group's capacity for intercultural competence." Denial, Defense, Reversal, Minimization, Acceptance, Adaptation, and Integration are dimensions highlighted in this framework. 22-(Taken from the Intercultural Development Inventory Manual Research by Dr. Mitchell Hammer and Dr. Milton Bennett, 1998, The Developmental Model of Intercultural Sensitivity (DMIS).

(1) List several cultural experiences that played a significant role in developing your worldviews and cultural lens:

(2) Have these experiences positively affected your current ability to accept and/or adapt to other cultures?

Basic Words of Communication

The ABC's of Diversity:

FINDING OTHERS WHO LOOK LIKE ME!

○ ○ ○

A major concern of organizations is not only how to find the best and most talented, but how to persuade that talent to believe in your organization's future. These are justifiable concerns. The best and most talented are available if you know where to look. However, as I have found when organizations make the assertion that the minority talent pool is dwindling or nonexistent, it is actually so much easier for corporate recruiters to pursue candidates who look just like them.

A closer look at this scenario is more revealing. If you send recruiters to new, more culturally sensitive environments where they haven't been before, it would only be natural that they may feel more uncomfortable at that location. That

87

Basic Words of Communication

The ABC's of Diversity:

"uncomfortableness" can easily be sensed by those who are verbally engaged by the recruiter, thus, both parties would be uncomfortable.

Regardless of whatever recruiting promises made, an invisible barrier may exist that questions the reality of the recruiter's spoken work. Hence, "I appreciate your offer but no thanks." Unfortunately, the recruiter may not even know such a barrier exists. I think this could be true for seasoned recruiters as well as those with a short longevity.

The answer is not in the questioning of the company's recruiting integrity, but in the cross-cultural competence level of the company's representative. Today's changing workforce has choices more than ever before. Twenty years ago those being recruited had to ignore culturally-related "light bulbs" that indicated a lack of sensitivity on a recruiter's part. Now, if something just doesn't feel right, the best and talented can simply refer to the next name on his/her list of possibilities.

Corporations have responded by helping recruiters better understand possible cultural biases that might be negatively affecting recruiting processes. An introspective process that acknowledges cultural biases improves the communication and the credibility of any corporate promise for change and inclusion. Cultural barriers can be addressed, a smoother delivery for diversity can be performed, and a higher recruiting rate for those "who don't look just like me" can take place.

This process should not be viewed as a negative statement of current HR practices, but as an enhancement suggestion only.

How tough is it to effectively recruit through untraditional sources?

———

FIVE MYTHS ABOUT LEADERSHIP

o o o

We constantly hear and read about the strengths attached to leadership. John C. Maxwell has this to say in his book entitled "The 21 Irrefutable Laws of Leadership:" There are plenty of misconceptions and myths that people embrace about leaders and leadership. Here are five common myths about leadership:

1. The Management Myth – a widespread misunderstanding is that leading and managing are one of the same. Up until a few years ago, books that

claimed to be about leadership were often really about management. The main difference between the two is that leadership is about influencing people to follow, while management focuses on maintaining systems and processes.

2. The Entrepreneur Myth – Frequently, people assume that all salespeople and entrepreneurs are leaders. That's not always the case. People may be buying what the salesman has to sell, but they are not following him. At best, he is able to persuade people for a moment, but he holds no long-term influence with them.

3. The Knowledge Myth – Most People, believing power is the essence of leadership, naturally assume that those who possess knowledge and intelligence are leaders. Yet, you can visit many university professors whose ability to think is higher than ever but have no ability to lead. Thus, IQ does not necessarily equate to leadership.

4. The Pioneer Myth – Another misconception is that anyone who is out in front of the crowd is a leader. Being first isn't always the same as leading. To be a leader, a person has to not only be out in front, but also have people intentionally coming behind him, following his lead, and acting on his vision.

5. The Position Myth – As mentioned earlier, the greatest misunderstanding about leadership is that people think it is based on position, but it is not. It's

not the position that makes the leader; it's the leader that makes the position.

John C. Maxwell's favorite leadership proverb: "He, who thinks he leads, but has no followers, is only taking a walk." If you can't influence others, they won't follow you. And, if they won't follow you, you're not a leader. Not matter what anybody else tells you, remember that leadership is influence – nothing more, nothing less."

23-(The 21 Irrefutable Laws of Leadership, John C. Maxwell, Chapter 2: The Laws of Influence, pg 14, Nelson Business Press, 1998.) pg 82;

GUIDELINES
FOR
ETHICAL
LEADERSHIP

ooo

Are Your Guidelines Acceptable?
"Learning to spot intolerable practices and to exercise good judgment when ethical conflicts arise requires practice. Creating a company culture that rewards ethical behavior is essential.

The following are guidelines for developing a global ethical perspective among managers. They are:

1. Treat corporate values and formal standards of conduct as absolute. Whatever ethical standards a company chooses, it then cannot waver on its principles either at home or abroad.

The ABC's of Diversity:

2. Design and implement conditions of engagement for suppliers and customers. Will your company do business with just any customer or supplier? What if that customer or supplier has questionable labor issues?

3. In host countries, support efforts to decrease institutional corruption. When a host country's tax system, import and export procedures, and procurement practices favor unethical players, companies must take some type of action. Some companies have moved to disclosing such instances in the media as a preventative measure.

4. Exercise moral imagination. Using moral imagination means resolving tensions responsibly and creatively. Find a manner in which you can enhance the perception of your company's ethical image and how it deals with the unethical advances made in global markets."

Allow foreign business units to help formulate ethical standards and interpret ethical issues. With the overarching intent to create a global ethics strategy, locally deployed, the diversity council's mandate is to provide ethics education and create local processes that will help managers in the company's foreign business units resolve ethical conflicts.

24-(The Harvard Business Review on Corporate Ethics. Guidelines for Ethical Leadership by Thomas Donaldson, pg 131, Harvard Business School Press, 2003)

GUTSY LEADERSHIP

o o o

Are you a Gutsy Leader?

Gutsy Leaders know in their hearts right from wrong. They are never without their moral compass. They respect diversity, recognize everyone is different and are aware that others may not share their values. Nonetheless, gutsy leaders are unwavering in living their values. One absolute value they will not compromise is character. Character refers to high ethical standards, empathy, compassion, and integrity. Unfortunately, winning at all cost seems to be a more important value than character. We see example after example of political, religious, and corporate leaders forgetting about honesty and ethics if it means not winning.

Winning, at times, has tremendous financial gain tied to it. Inflating figures; engaging in unethical partnerships; kickback schemes; misusing insider information; destroying damaging evidence; and, any number of other behaviors that have been commonplace in the business world. Gutsy Leaders won't compromise for the sake of profit. How Gutsy are you?

25-(Gutsy Leadership: A Common Sense Workbook on Leadership Development, Leon T. Lanier, Sr., Renaissance Publishers, Inc, 2003)

Would your workplace embrace Gutsy Leaders or see them as a threat?

The ABC's of Diversity:

GUTSY TALK

○ ○ ○

"In an effort to optimize the educational concepts associated with the workplace, the environment must engage in "gutsy" talk. Gutsy talk occurs when everyone in the organization can safely identify issues that affect their ability to do their best work…. without fear of retribution. Gutsy talk must occur in an open, non-judgmental environment if effective results are sought. I think we all agree that one of the most criticized workplace issues is poor communication. It occurs everywhere, including all levels of leadership.

Gutsy talk, implemented correctly, addresses serious communication concerns like: half-truths, lack of communication, sugar-coated communications, outright lies, fear of communication, and miscommunication. Gutsy leaders, however, are not afraid to engage in gutsy conversations. In fact, it's a most valuable tool. Answer the following questions: Why are you ready to become a gutsy leader? Can you respect diverse opinions? Do you shut down if your opinion is found unfavorable to others? Do you listen objectively? If you can respond to these questions honestly, you may be able to engage in gutsy talk.
(*26*-Gutsy Leadership: A Common Sense Workbook on Leadership Development, Leon T. Lanier, Sr., Renaissance Publishers, Inc. pg 51, 2003)
Can you be totally honest with others without feeling guilty? And, without fear of retribution?

Harmful "Phrases"

o o o

Our normal understanding of language is derived from our community worldviews, interpreting and reinterpreting our everyday conversations, and through acceptance and/or denial of healthy dialogue and debate from others both similar to us and not.

As this process matures our social/cultural perceptions of our verbal rights and wrongs, we eventually take these communication skills with us to new cultural communities expecting only the best. No intentional malice is intended but that value can be too subjective when it comes to phrases that may be viewed as offensive.

"Some of my best friends are……"
"You people……..."
"Those people….."

are examples listed under this section of "harmful phrases."

When these words are used in a conversation, the interpretation of how they have been used and what they really mean may vary. They may vary based on which community the speaker/listener learned his/her communication skills.

From an African American perspective, I am of the opinion that such phrases can be demeaning when used to describe a possible cultural relationship. They may suggest a social class difference where one class is better than another. They may imply that one social class is talking down to another as it refers to the latter. And, it may minimize the value of the conversation even if the speaker is attempting to make a positive cultural connection - one that validates a credible reality of his/her cultural values.

It's important to understand that harmful phrases may be used without any negative intention. The key learning in this instance is to recognize that there will be worldview differences between the person speaking and the person listening.

List several other phrases that may be perceived as offensive in nature.

The ABC's of Diversity:

HOMOPHOBIA

o o o

Fear of or contempt for lesbians and gay men; behavior based on such a feeling. An irrational fear of, aversion to, or discrimination against homosexuality or homosexuals prejudice against (fear or dislike of) homosexual people and homosexuality.

HOW
AMBIGUOUS
BEHAVIORS
AFFECT
THE
WORKPLACE

o o o

The uncertainty attached to unclear messages of communication as it spreads throughout the workplace tends to have an unwelcome, negative element of surprise. This unknown causes worry, anxiety, and a tremendous amount of frustration – warranted or not. These elements can do nothing but act as barriers that prevent employees from bringing their best and brightest mindsets through the company's front door each morning. In "Driving Fear Out of the Workplace, it acknowledges that "In cases such as this, people frequently do not know what to do. They grope in darkness and worry about what will befall them. All they know is that they do not know. This leads to speculation, concern, and worst-case thinking."

"Unfortunately, when reliable information is not available, many people rely on the cycle of mistrust. This cycle is a ready reservoir of explanations for a mixed message, lack of feedback, or indirect communication. We tend to encourage people to decipher in a negative way the who, what, why and how. This lack of information combined with negative assumptions and mistrust cause employees to be afraid." 2.

27-(Kathleen Ryan & Daniel Ostreich; Driving Fear out of the Workplace: Creating a High Trust High Performance Organization; Second Edition, pg 190; Chapter 11, Reduce Ambiguous Behavior; Jossey-Bass, 1998)

The ABC's of Diversity:

HOW
TO
MEASURE
SUCCESS

o o o

A caveat if there ever was one – the strategy for measuring the effectiveness of any diversity intervention is one of patience. The path forward is a long-term process and not a short-term project. Seeking to measure cultural personality changes, based on another's timeframe, can be asking for trouble.

Each employee can and will change but on their own motivation. Whether such can happen immediately, monthly or yearly is based equally on each employee's ethnocentric experiences and their ability to practice the handling of newly discovered biases – personal and otherwise. Our cultural lens took a lifetime to develop. The only pressure was to understand ourselves – not others.

I do think that a specific kind of measurement can occur. I tend to be in favor of random, confidentially obtained pre-test / post-test measurements that seek to understand how much interest an employee has in understanding another's culture. A lot can be done with the collected pre-test data in terms of finding the real pulse of an organization. By simply asking 25 questions, attitudes about workplace

Basic Words of Communication

The ABC's of Diversity:

respect, inclusion, and leadership commitment can be captured. Participating in the pre-test is not mandatory and, by just asking for such feedback, news of a positive, inclusive diversity initiative spreads rapidly throughout the organization.

Your organization's personnel will allow a process of inclusion to develop its own speed. Once inclusion becomes the buzzword for change, employees will not expect that change to occur overnight. They will, however, expect a process – regardless of size – to have started. When this mindset begins, future change is expected and some kind of diversity process needs to begin "right now" – not that any results have to be collected next week.

Once any process is endorsed by those it's to serve, a reasonable amount of patience is automatically attached to its successful mission.

What are several "indirect" successes, culturally speaking, that can be measured in your workplace?

The ABC's of Diversity:

HUMAN CAPITAL

o o o

The value of human capital?

Human Capital includes personnel with longevity as well as those candidates most recently hired. In his recent and provocative book, Intellectual Capital: The New Wealth of Organizations (1997), Thomas Stewart points out that "knowledge has become the primary raw material and result of economic activity and that organizational intelligence – smart people working in smart ways – has moved from a supporting role to a starring one."

He emphasizes human capital and defines it as "the capabilities of the individuals required to provide solutions to customers. He adds that human capital matters because it is the source of innovation and renewal, whether from brainstorming in a lab or new leads found in a sale's rep's little black book".

28-(Driving Fear Out of the Workplace, Kathleen Ryan and Daniel Oestreich, Chapter 16, pg 294, Jossey-Bass Publishers, 1998)

o o o

Are you an inclusive person?

Inclusion is a term used to describe an organizational culture in which everyone is fully and respectfully involved in work functions and daily activities. In diversity-related terms, it may be the foundation for exceptional levels of service and profitability. Creating an environment where everyone's individual talent is engaged and fully utilized is the desired intervention.

(1) What is your definition of Inclusion?

(2) Is everyone respectfully involved in work functions at your workplace? If so, give some examples.

INDIVIDUAL CONTRIBUTOR

○ ○ ○

Every employee, regardless of the level of corporate responsibility, is an individual contributor and should be treated and respected as a valuable part of the corporate environment.

Are you recognized as a valued individual contributor? Why or why not?

INTERPERSONAL ORIENTATION

○ ○ ○

Interpersonal orientation is a focus that allows an observer to determine whether a person is more concerned with achieving good social relations or with accomplishing a task.

The ABC's of Diversity:

INTROSPECTION

o o o

Do you know why you are the way you are?
A powerful term diversity leaders must understand
throughout any change process is "introspection." Defined
correctly, introspection forms the personal foundation for
seeking understandings of inner values and beliefs. Webster
says that this is the examination of one's thoughts and
feelings; a looking inward and the process of self ownership;
and, the inspection of one's own thoughts and behaviors.

What I find most irresistible about introspection is its
strength. It identifies underlying issues and deals with those
that drive our behaviors… good and bad behaviors that
eventually make up our leadership persona, worldviews, and
cultural lens. Any effort made to move an organization
towards respect and inclusion needs to begin that process by
making sure each individual contributor understands their
ethnocentric self. It is through individual ownership of self
that masses can begin the long road of discovery.

29-(Gutsy Leadership: a Common Sense Workbook on Leadership Development, Leon T.
Lanier, Renaissance Publishers, 2003)

The ABC's of Diversity:

Lanier Diversity Consultants

CULTURE
CHANGE
PHILOSOPHY

Diversity Power of I^3
Introspection + Inclusion = Innovation
Driving Human Capital

The very essence of understanding culture, any culture, is to effectively identify and communicate the value of life's ever-changing worldviews on a progressive and proactive basis. This sounds simple but is it really? How do we engage, promote and measure inclusive behavior on a consistent basis? What's the next ideological formula for driving measurable culture change? These are tough questions that require even tougher answers.

Basic Words of Communication

The ABC's of Diversity:

Lanier Diversity Consultants, Inc.'s workplace philosophy realizes that corporate America has progressed to a cultural plateau where "Innovation" is the next logical ideology. Supporting this reality, we believe that an individual's best work can be attained by: (1) better understanding and taking ownership of their introspective selves; (2) coming to a workplace environment where respect and inclusion is actively being embedded in the organization; and, (3) observing accountability at all levels of the organization whenever the opportunity exists.

We truly support the three key features explained above. We feel that positive culture change will consistently drive the value of human capital to its highest potential on a daily basis. In return, this philosophy should stimulate higher levels of innovative thinking across all cultural barriers. Respectful rights and privileges of the "total organization" can now be addressed under one corporate initiative ... Innovation!"

It is our opinion that assumptions made from previous historical mandates have not totally met their desired goals. As an example, it was assumed that Affirmative Action Programs (backed by legal sanctions) would lead to a level playing field in America. It was assumed that Equal Employment Opportunity Compliance Laws would create workplace balances. And, it was assumed that corporate diversity mandates, business case results, and "just do the right thing" attitudes would drive workplace respect to

Basic Words of Communication

The ABC's of Diversity:

socially acceptable levels. I think each helped but not to the extent this country expected. Unfortunately, my workplace experiences have found that even though workplace respect has significantly increased throughout corporate America, the aforementioned assumptions still fell short of culturally-related desires.

Several reasons for the above shortfalls may be that: (1) culture change, ethnocentric experiences, and freedom of choice are all humanistic in nature; (2) personal feelings cannot be pushed on society as a whole nor mandated exclusively from a boardroom; and, (3) although individual mindsets can more effectively take ownership of their own biases, it's much harder to drive desired behaviors of others across cultural barriers just because "it's the right thing to do... based on a cultural foundation as 'you' see it." Respecting the rights of your fellow man requires much, much more.

The Diversity Power of I^3: Introspection + Inclusion = Innovation is a critical part of the LDC change philosophy.

(1) I^1 represents the 1st degree of understanding. This degree focuses on developing human capital at the introspection level. Introspection helps individual contributors understand their worldviews or cultural lens. This degree also seeks spatial learning opportunities that practice ownership of new biases. And, lastly, it directly focuses on developing what's

Basic Words of Communication

The ABC's of Diversity:

needed to keep minds and behaviors at the cutting edge for enhanced levels of innovative thinking;

(2) I^2 represents the 2nd degree of understanding. This degree involves acknowledging and valuing corporate inclusion policies and practices. Introspective work on ourselves would be lost energy if the workplace was not open to better communication skills or we didn't seek more overall accountability to mandated policies and procedures; and,

(3) I^3 represents the 3rd degree. It seeks to increase the value of human capital to a point where each employee's personal initiative is the motivating force that drives his/her creativity at the workplace every day. Innovative human capital requires a freedom of thought mindset, communication skills to correctly speak that freedom, and a workplace that places a consistent value on inclusion qualities – all for the sake of enhancing business case value.

Lanier Diversity Consultants work hard to transition the value of previously implemented diversity and inclusion strategies forward to the next plateau of understanding. We acknowledge the strengths of introspective work, previously accepted corporate policies and initiatives, and the environment's desire to express creative mindset's to the fullest on a daily basis.

The ABC's of Diversity:

LDC's change philosophy drives personal creativity to a higher level, blesses the results of innovative human capital, and positively influences bottom-line results.

(If you would like more information on this philosophy please contact LanierDiversityConsultants.com)

LEADERSHIP

o o o

Leadership is simply "getting things done through people!" That's my definition of leadership and I have not changed it over the last twenty years. This doesn't mean I haven't thought about changing it many times but the bottom line is that it keeps coming back to the same definition – especially in a cultural setting. Great leadership inspires, empowers, motivates and challenges all that one can be; interprets the organization's vision; makes the company's vision come to life; acts selfishly for the good of all in the organization; exudes character and compassion; builds community; empowers others to become a part of the corporate vision; understands creativity and sometimes unpopular positioning; and faithfully makes inclusive decisions because it's simply the right thing to do.

Basic Words of Communication

The ABC's of Diversity:

Stephen R. Covey's defines leadership as "communicating to people their worth and potential so clearly that they come to see in themselves." Now, think about this definition. Isn't this the essence of the kind of leadership that influences and truly endures? To communicate the worth and potential of others so clearly, so powerful and so consistently that they really come to see it in themselves is to set in motion to process of seeing, doing, and becoming."

30-(The 8th Habit from Effectiveness to Greatness, Stephen R. Covey, pg 98, Free Press of Simon and Schuster, inc, 2004.)

What's your definition of leadership?

LEAN MANUFACTURING

o o o

Lean manufacturing is a management philosophy that assumes that any manufacturing structure that does not add value to the total production process is a wasteful process.

Basic Words of Communication

The ABC's of Diversity:

In a cultural sense, when employees are unhappy with the workplace environment, they probably are not spending one hundred percent of their time being productively efficient.

Production time lost, whether it's in thought, talking on the telephone, increased sick time, unwarranted lengthened lunch breaks, or even time spent complaining to HR – if eliminated or reduced, could positively contribute to a more efficient or leaner manufacturing process.

Lean manufacturing acknowledges this waste. Introducing a total team effort, it seeks to develop a process that more effectively utilizes the total skills of the team and to perform in the best interest of the organization.

Can lean manufacturing be utilized in your organization?

LISTENING SKILLS

o o o

The Truth about Listening?
The hardest part of listening may not be about listening at all. It may be about your proper response during and after the listening has been shared.

The ABC's of Diversity:

The most common misunderstanding is decision-making by the listener. As the personal information is being shared, there are many openings for the listener to "fix" whatever the problem may be. As I have learned over the years, the best way to "fix" the listener's issues is not to "fix" them at all. The best fix is to lend an ear and let the speaker be heard.

Does the word empathy come to mind? The listener's greatest joy is to be heard and to be told that an acceptance of their perspectives has been given an equal ear. Nothing more. Nothing less. Actually, to do more creates the problem of…. questioning the quality of your listening skills.

Have you found this perspective to be accurate? Why? Why not?

Basic Words of Communication

MAGNITUDE
OF
THE GAP

o o o

Many leaders have an impression that they understand the wants and needs of their employees. They also think they have a good ideal where the organization stands on cultural issues. Yet, time after time, the results from organizational audits reveal this assumption not to be the case.

The level of workplace sensitivity and understanding tends to be acknowledged as an awakening of sorts to top management. This level of misunderstanding is known as the magnitude of the gap – i.e. the reality of your workplace.

(1) *As a manager, are you really in tune with your organization?*

(2) *How far is your organization from where it wants to be?*

The ABC's of Diversity:

MANAGEMENT

∘ ∘ ∘

…focuses on processes, systems, and procedures to insure that rules are followed. Management differs from Managers in that managers oversee a specific function. Leaders, on the other hand, usually focus on doing the right thing while managers usually focus on doing things right.

What is your definition of management?

MICRO-INEQUITIES

∘ ∘ ∘

Hidden and/or discreet non-inclusive actions and behaviors that create barriers to a respectful, inclusive workplace where all individual contributors feel valued by the organization. Small exclusive behaviors that could negatively affect the perceived fairness in any organization. An example of a micro-inequity could be a known or unknown personal bias against other cultures that somehow shows up when evaluating women and minorities. A systematic exclusionary issue that is hard to pinpoint.

(1) List several micro-inequities attached to your environment.

MINIMIZATION

o o o

In a cultural context, "Issues in Minimization indicate that you have gotten beyond feeling that other cultures pose a threat to your own. Your experience is that people from other cultures are pretty much like you, under the surface. You are quite aware that other cultures exist all around you and you may know something about cultural differences in customs, celebrations, etc. You do not denigrate other cultures and you seek to avoid stereotypes by treating every person as an individual or by treating other people, as you would like to be treated."

"In an educational or business setting, you probably feel supportive of equal opportunity and colorblind recruitment, but you may not be certain whether or how the organization should change to accommodate more diversity."
3f-(taken from the Intercultural Development Inventory Manual by Dr. Mitch Hammer and Dr. Milton Bennett, 1998).

The ABC's of Diversity:

Have you minimized in any instance recently? Think about it.

Multi-Cultural Organization

o o o

An organization in which employees of mixed backgrounds, experiences, and cultures can contribute and achieve their full potential for the benefit of both themselves and the organization.

The ABC's of Diversity:

MYTHS ABOUT THE AFRICAN AMERICAN MALE

o o o

"It's important in today's workplace to develop the level of understanding needed to build good relationships when associates are from another culture – whether you are a new entry-level employee or a top executive. A major key is to learn about an associate's culture and get a feel for his or her background. The more skilled you become at interpreting an individual's actions against the back-drop of his or her culture, the greater success both of you can achieve through working together.

Most of the myths and stereotypes about African Americans are false or distorted partial truths. In fact, most stem from the legacy of slavery and segregation that is unique to this American subgroup. In order to justify slavery, a practice that is quite incompatible with the American ideals of human freedom and equality, some Euro-Americans created degrading stereotypes of Africans. Such beliefs are passed along from generation to generation and truly die hard.

The ABC's of Diversity:

Although the proportion of Euro-Americans who hold the more extreme stereotypes is continually declining, certain beliefs are still held by the majority. Some stereotypes still held are that: African Americans are more violent than Whites; Are less intelligent than Whites; Are more likely to prefer to live off welfare; They blame everyone else but themselves for their problems; and, They tend to be resentful troublemakers. The bottom line here is that we have some work to do on changing these beliefs and attitudes. Remember, myths are sayings or stories used to bind together the thoughts of a group and promote social action.

To get to know what it's like to be an African American, you must understand the stereotypes they deal with every time they leave the family or community circle, or turn on the television for that matter. To bridge the divisive walls these stereotypes hold in place, you must know what they are, know other realities that balance or refute them, and move beyond myths to a more realistic view of the African American community."

32(taken from Diversity Success Strategies, Chapter 6, pg 128, written by Norma-Carr Ruffino, Butterworth/Heinemann Publishers, 1999)

Any additional myths about African Americans not recognized above?

MYTHS
ABOUT
THE
ASIAN AMERICAN

o o o

"People who have taken the time and effort to learn something about Asian Americans. Their values and issues, say they've boosted their ability to work productively with these associates. Most of the myths and stereotypes about Asian Americans are false or distorted partial truths. In fact, most stem from the belief that Asian Americans are too foreign to really understand. Several myths and stereotypes about Asian Americans are: that they tend to retain their foreign ways and it's difficult for them to fit in; Asian Americans are unemotional and inscrutable; Asian Americans are too passive and too polite to be managers; they can't seem to master the English language thus they have communication problems; and, although good in the technical field, lack creative leadership skills."

33(Taken from Diversity Success Strategies, Chapter , pg 156, written by Norma-Carr Ruffino, Butterworth/Heinemann Publishers, 1999)

Any additional myths about Asian Americans not mentioned above?

The ABC's of Diversity:

MYTHS ABOUT LATIN AMERICANS

o o o

"Latino American communities include people from many countries. While most of their values and customs are woven from common Latino threads, each country also has its own unique design. However, you already know the necessity of dealing with each person as a unique individual from a particular cultural background. Some typical myths about Latino Americans are: They are too passive and lacking in conviction to be good leaders; They are too emotional and excitable to fill leadership positions; The men are too macho and the women easily intimidated; and, They are qualified only for menial jobs."

"These myths stem from misunderstandings about the ways certain cultural values and customs affect Latino Americans' attitudes and actions. Cultural style, such as passivity or politeness, is often misinterpreted as leadership inadequacy, such as the inability to take initiative and be firm. The ultimate goal is to appreciate Latino Americans' unique value to the workplace and to strengthen workplace unity."
34(taken from Diversity Success Strategies, Chapter 8, pg 184, written by Norma-Carr Ruffino, Butterworth/Heinemann Publishers, 1999)

Basic Words of Communication

The ABC's of Diversity:

Any additional myths about Latin Americans not mentioned?

MYTHS ABOUT GLBTs

○ ○ ○

"Gay men, lesbians, and bisexuals, sometimes referred to collectively as gay persons, are often called the invisible minority because they don't look different from others in their ethnic group. To become comfortable with gay associates, and in turn to build good working relationships, you need to get a feel for their lifestyle, community, and background. The more skilled you become at interpreting individual associates' actions against the backdrop of their background, the greater your chances of working well together."

"Most myths and stereotypes stem from a belief that gay persons perversely choose an unnatural sexual orientation. The American Psychological Association has concluded from research that this belief is unfounded. Yet, GLBT's still face the following stereotypes: Gays cluster in certain occupations; People who associate with gays are probably

125

Basic Words of Communication

gay themselves; Gays in sensitive or high-level jobs are security risks; Gay men act feminine and gay women act masculine; and gay persons are a bad influence on children. Again, these are the stereotypes gays must deal with every day."

35-(taken from Diversity Success Strategies, Chapter 9, pg 211, written by Norma-Carr Ruffino, Butterworth/Heinemann Publishers, 1999)

Any additional myths about GLBT's?

MYTHS, LEGENDS
&
SYMBOLS

o o o

Stories that bind together the thoughts of a group and promotes coordinated social action – more symbolic than factual.

List several of the above categories as they apply to your organization.

ℕ𝔸𝕋𝕀𝕆ℕ𝔸𝕃 𝕆ℝ𝕀𝔾𝕀ℕ 𝔻𝕀𝕊ℂℝ𝕀𝕄𝕀ℕ𝔸𝕋𝕀𝕆ℕ

o o o

Whether an employee or job applicant's ancestry is Mexican, Ukrainian, Filipino, Arab, American Indian, or any other nationality, he or she is entitled to the same employment opportunities as anyone else.

EEOC enforces the federal prohibition against national origin discrimination in employment under Title VII of the Civil Rights Act of 1964, which covers employers with fifteen (15) or more employees.

The ABC's of Diversity:

NATURAL
WORK
TEAMS

o o o

"It's extremely important to allow the confidentiality of self-assessments to remain the discreet choice of the individual. However, based on past experiences, effective learning curves are lower when learning is not conducted in a shared natural work team environment.

When learning takes place in a natural work team, natural team discussions tend to enhance the scrutiny of key behaviors in a positive manner. As further clarification, instant feedback from peer groups have proven to be a tremendously effective tool as long as the feedback is communicated in respectful, supporting ways.

As a caveat, natural work teams should eliminate any possibility of "buddy or pal" interferences. It's important to have safe, trustful (and, discreet) learning environments, Peer group feedback, when communicated in safe learning environments, enables individually targeted improvement. The obvious level found within the natural work team can measure a person's rate of progression. This measurement allows individuals to evaluate what they have learned, address their personal levels of need, and improve at their own acceptable pace.

The ABC's of Diversity:

As their personal journey unfolds – personal growth expands. The evaluation process should help leaders discover and adjust to hidden attitudes and values that may be barriers to personal transformation. Subsequently, by adding the value of gutsy talk discussions and better listening skills to this equation, greater leadership growth should emerge at an individual pace."

36-(Gutsy Leadership: a Common Sense Workbook on Leadership Development, Leon T. Lanier, pg 30-32, Renaissance Publishers, 2003)

ORGANIZATIONAL BEHAVIOR

o o o

A field of study that investigates the impact that individuals, groups, and structure have on behavior within organizations for the purpose of applying such knowledge toward improving an organization's effectiveness.

ORGANIZATIONAL CHANGE

o o o

The intentional attempt by management to improve the overall performance of individuals, groups, and the organization by altering the organization's structure, behavior and technology.

The ABC's of Diversity:

PREJUDICE

○ ○ ○

Workplace prejudice is still active in our culture. Surveys, such as those done by the National Opinion Research Center, "indicate that stereotypes are still prevalent and that most of the Euro-American men who run the workplace believe that other ethnic groups are less intelligent, less hard working, less likely to be self supporting, more violence prone, and less patriotic than they are. The US Glass Ceiling Commission has stated in their research that prejudice (sexism, racism, ethnic prejudice, and other 'isms) is the biggest advancement barrier that diverse employees face today."

37-(taken from Diversity Success Strategies, Chapter 3, pg 66, written by Norma-Carr Ruffino, Butterworth/Heinemann Publishers, 1999)

Does prejudice exist in your workplace? If not, what proactive practices assisted in that transition?

If yes, how does it manifest itself?

PRESTO!
GREAT
LEADERS

o o o

Introspection is only one of many concepts that help determine future stages of leadership transformation. Unfortunately, there isn't a special, magical, leadership dust on the market that can be sprinkled over a group and... presto! – Great leaders shall emerge. For quality leadership to occur, emerging candidates must acknowledge and take ownership of personal barriers to biases, attitudes, and values found within others and, even more importantly... found within themselves.

38-(Gutsy Leadership: A Common Sense Workbook on Leadership Development, 1st Edition, Leon T. Lanier, Sr., Chapter IV, pg 45, renaissance Publishers, 2002)

PROACTIVE
CHANGE

o o o

Proactive change is a type of change that occurs when an organization's managers conclude that a change would be "desirable", as opposed to being "necessary."

PROACTIVE MANAGEMENT

o o o

Proactive management is a management style in which decision makers anticipate problems and take affirmative steps to minimize those problems, rather than waiting until a problem occur before taking action.

o o o

"Racism is typically a problem in societies such as the United States, where there is a predominant 'majority group' and one or more cultural subgroups. People often use the term racism in discussions of prejudice, which raises the question, "How do I know when I'm dealing with someone of another race, and how can I be sure what race they represent?"

39-(taken from Diversity Success Strategies, Chapter 3, pg 66, written by Norma-Carr Ruffino, Butterworth/Heinemann Publishers, 1999)

Racism can be defined in a variety of ways.

What is your definition of racism? List several examples of how you've observed it personally and professionally.

The ABC's of Diversity:

RESPECTING CULTURAL DIFFERENCES

○ ○ ○

Respecting cultural differences is an organizational plateau that seeks a higher level of workplace understanding. Yet, there still lingers a perception that to "respect" another's cultural difference means that one has to also "accept" them as their own. This perception is far from the truth.

Respecting cultural differences only means that you "recognize and respect" the right for others to relate to their cultural lens and/or worldviews... whatever they may be.

It is not necessary for you to accept another's worldview or behavior "as your own."

It is only necessary to respect another's cultural lens as a right afforded to them without having to seek validation from others.

The ABC's of Diversity:

REVERSAL

○ ○ ○

Reversal, as described in a cultural worldview context by the Intercultural Development Inventory (IDI), indicates "that you have a largely positive view of an adopted culture or other cultures in general and a somewhat negative opinion of your own. However, your understanding of the adopted culture may be based on positive stereotypes.

As an example, as a member of a dominant ethnic group who is concerned with ethnic oppression, you may have disavowed your own ethnic roots in favor of being "one with" members of the oppressed group."
40-(taken from the Intercultural Development Inventory Manual by Dr. Mitch Hammer and Dr. Milton Bennett, 1998).

The ABC's of Diversity:

SELF-EMPOWERMENT

o o o

In a cultural sense?

"When it is said that leadership is a choice, it basically means you can choose the level of initiative you want to exercise in response to the question, 'What is the best I can do under the circumstances?'" Stephen R. Covey says in his book... "The 8th Habit: From Effectiveness to Greatness," that there are 7 levels of self-empowerment and you choose which level of initiative to use based on how far the task lies within your circle of influence. The 7 levels are: (1) <u>Wait until told</u> to do something; (2) take the initiative and "<u>ask</u>" if something needs to be done; (3) <u>Make a recommendation</u> that something needs to be done; (4) <u>I intend to</u> do something about it; (5) <u>Do it and report immediately</u>; (6) <u>Do it and report periodically</u>; and (7), <u>Just Do it</u>. It takes judgment and wisdom to know what level of initiative to exercise – what you should do; how you should do it; when you should do it; and, why you should do it.

Taking initiative is a form of self-empowerment. No leader has empowered you. The organizational structure hasn't empowered you. Your job description hasn't empowered you. Your job description hasn't empowered you. You empower yourself based on the issue or the problem or the challenge at hand.

Culture change is a very easy phenomenon to openly talk about: yet, a very hard initiative to introduce to the organization. The topic of empowerment keeps coming back to your level of leadership – within your personal and professional circle of influence."
4f(Stephen R. Covey, The 8ᵗʰ Habit, Chapter 7, The Voice of Influence, pg 132, 142, Simon and Schuster, 2005)

SENSITIVITY TRAINING

o o o

Sensitivity Training is a form of educational experience that stresses the emotional dynamics of self-development training. The training may be highly structured or highly unstructured to permit the participants to learn more about their strengths and weaknesses concerning cultural differences.

SEXISM

○ ○ ○

"Sexism is prejudice based on gender and is said by some to be the root of all prejudice and discrimination. As children we literally begin learning this form of inequality from the cradle. It doesn't involve a majority and minority, since men and women are relatively equal in number.   However, women in all countries are a minority in economic and political arenas and have fewer rights and privileges than men."
42-(taken from Diversity Success Strategies, Chapter 3, pg 66, written by Norma-Carr Ruffino, Butterworth/Heinemann Publishers, 1999)

Identify examples of sexism you have observed in your environment:

SEXUAL HARASSMENT

o o o

"Sexual harassment is a form of sex discrimination that violates <u>Title VII of the Civil Rights Act of 1964</u>. Title VII applies to employers with 15 or more employees, including state and local governments. It also applies to employment agencies and to labor organizations, as well as to the federal government. Unwelcome sexual advances, requests for sexual favors, and other verbal or physical conduct of a sexual nature constitute sexual harassment when this conduct explicitly or implicitly affects an individual's employment, unreasonably interferes with an individual's work performance, or creates an intimidating, hostile, or offensive work environment.

Sexual harassment can occur in a variety of circumstances, including but not limited to the following: The victim as well as the harasser may be a woman or a man. The victim does not have to be of the opposite sex. The harasser can be the victim's supervisor, an agent of the employer, a supervisor in another area, a co-worker, or a non-employee. The victim does not have to be the person harassed but could be anyone affected by the offensive conduct. Unlawful sexual harassment may occur without economic injury to or discharge of the victim. The harasser's conduct must be unwelcome. It is helpful for the victim to inform the harasser directly that the conduct is unwelcome and must stop. The victim should use any employer complaint mechanism or grievance system available.

When investigating allegations of sexual harassment, EEOC looks at the whole record: the circumstances, such as the nature of the sexual advances, and the context in which the alleged incidents occurred. A determination on the allegations is made from the facts on a case-by-case basis. Prevention is the best tool to eliminate sexual harassment in the workplace.

Employers are encouraged to take steps necessary to prevent sexual harassment from occurring. They should clearly communicate to employees that sexual harassment will not be tolerated. They can do so by providing sexual harassment training to their employees and by establishing an effective complaint or grievance process and taking immediate and appropriate action when an employee complains. It is also unlawful to retaliate against an individual for opposing employment practices that discriminate based on sex or for filing a discrimination charge, testifying, or participating in any way in an investigation, proceeding, or litigation under Title VII."

Sexual harassment occurs not only when initiated by men but also when initiated by women. Give an example of each.

SOCIAL RESPONSIBILITY

○ ○ ○

The expectation that companies should act in the public interest and contribute to the solution of social and ecological problems.

Do you think corporations should be more socially responsible than individuals?

SPATIAL LEARNING

○ ○ ○

Spatial learning occurs when learning is directly aligned to each individual's ability to understand the personal work; the amount of time allotted to practice that personal work in the real world; and, after a personal evaluation process, the ability to again practice it in a workplace.

The building block principle of learning is the foundation.

STEREOTYPING

o o o

The belief that all members of a cultural group behave the same way.

What was the last stereotypical comment you made?

STRUCTURAL INTERVENTION

o o o

Changing the structure of the organization so that people can develop new approaches for dealing with others on the job.

SUGAR-
COATED
COMMUNICATIONS

○ ○ ○

This term relates to the inability to discuss issues of respect and inclusion honestly. Many times when an organization seeks to disseminate a corporate mandate that it will no longer tolerate a non-respectful workplace, it disseminates a message that has a low-risk level of offensiveness.

Have you ever "minimized the severity" of a message you had to deliver to a group you were leading?

———

SUSTAINABLE COMPETITIVE ADVANTAGE

o o o

Advantages over your competitors that can be sustained over time. A workplace where all employees are treated with respect can be considered a sustainable competitive advantage if your competitors do not seek similar workplace values.

List several other sustainable competitive advantages found in your organization.

SYSTEMATIC EXCLUSION

o o o

Think of a non-inclusive, multi-cultural work environment where trust is never mentioned, respect among workplace cultures has to be earned on a daily basis and fades just as fast, and the need to be cross-culturally competent never crosses anyone's mind. Now think about the promotional evaluation process that takes place between subordinate and supervisor within this environment. How can a fair process of upward mobility ever occur? And, exactly who's responsible if it never does – the employee who never voices his/her concerns or the supervisors for never seeking a more inclusive policy?

In circumstances like these, it's hard to point the finger at any one layer of the process for its shortcomings. At first glance, the supervisor appears responsible because of his/her connection to management. Yet, once we find that people skills were never a supervisor's strong point, we can eliminate him/her for not knowing what they did not know. HR becomes a target until its revealed that their training budgets were slashed and delivering better people skills were the first classes eliminated. We can go on and on but I think you get the message. Systematic exclusion occurs when an organization's leadership commitment doesn't seek accountability at every level. In the above scenario, even if no pressure comes from employees about the fairness of any process, the supervisor at every level has a responsibility to make things happen. The fact that no one takes the lead does not diminish the responsibility. And, blaming could be directed totally across the management spectrum.

This broad range of a "leadership non-accountability" is a valid portrayal of what systematic exclusion is all about. It is not far enough for responsible parties to acknowledge that "someone" should have done a better job. You correct this by making sure every level is held accountable or the wrong message will be perceived – one of no commitment.

TALENT MANAGEMENT

o o o

An approach to sourcing strategy, developing and promoting the top executives and those likely to replace them; includes a number of human resources processes including hiring, retention, succession planning, development, assessment, coaching, and mentoring.

TASK-MOTIVATED LEADERSHIP...

A leadership style in which the manager tends to describe his or her least preferred coworker in an unfavorable light. Such a leader is primarily involved in task controlling and managing and is less concerned with the human relations aspects of the job.

THE TIPPING POINT

ooo

A Cultural Association?

"The Tipping Point is the 'biography' of a very simple idea. It's the best way to understand the emergence of fashion trends, the ebb and flow of crime waves... or, any number of mysterious changes in ideas, products and behaviors that mark everyday life.

The Tipping Point generally has three characteristics. The first is that a minor incident can be effectively contagious. The second is that little causes can have big effects. And, the third characteristic is that change happens not gradually but at one dramatic moment. The latter is the most important because it is the principle that makes sense of the first two and that permits the greatest insight into why modern change happens the way it does. Thus, the name given to that one dramatic moment when everything can change all at once is, in fact, The Tipping Point."

Understanding America's changing workplace can be described as a Tipping Point of sorts because culture change, as a "biography of an idea," has tremendously affected this country. Not just the demographic numbers and how they

The ABC's of Diversity:

will change by year 2020, but the ideology of change that we must now ascribe to. We can look around and see the changing faces of America's workplace, We experience the cultural differences and acknowledge that we just might be acting in an "exclusive" manner after all. Somehow we may recognize that belonging to this new cultural ideology is actually important to us. The Tipping Point, in this regard, is the awareness and the importance to being cross-culturally competent – personally and professionally.

Efforts to move any organization forward starts with a better understanding of self and then spreads to the organization. Thus, the moment I better understand who I am, including any of my cultural biases. I have entered that dramatic moment where I now "get it!" This respect I now must give to others came from the smallest cultural seed. Thus, the key to getting people to change their behavior sometimes lies with the smallest details of their immediate situation. This is a perfect example of The Tipping Point.

43-(The Tipping Point, Malcolm Gladwell, Chapter 1, pg 28, Back Bay Books/Little, Brown & Company, 2002)

Has there been a minor issue that has created a major impact in your organization? An issue or occurrence at first thought to be minor yet grew to major implications and significance?

The ABC's of Diversity:

THE
TRANSPARENT
COMPANY

○ ○ ○

What is a Transparent Company?

"A transparent company can be defined as one that's rooted in core values, based on the greatest good for the greatest number of people, with a leader who believes in doing the right thing at all times – no matter what the consequences. That means following the rules, no matter how boring that may sound, and telling it like it is, as hard as that may seem. The transparent company fosters a culture of openness and inclusion, and therefore is able to adapt to unexpected shifts in market conditions by simply doing the right thing.

There are three principles a transparent company must have: (1) a leader who believes in telling the whole truth… The Whole Truth; (2) A method of establishing and sustaining a values-based corporate culture (values are simply a list of things that are important to you); and, (3) employees who are "people-people" (service-oriented/team players)."

Take the transparency test:

1. Have you ever hidden a mistake from a superior or colleague?
2. Have you ever failed to disclose a product bug, defect, shortcoming, etc?

154

Basic Words of Communication

The ABC's of Diversity:

3. Have you ever expensed a lunch or dinner when it wasn't exclusively for business?
4. Does you organization have a written cultural contract?
5. Can you list all of the items on the contract right now, without reading it?
6. Are you accessible to every employee you manage, and if you are the CEO, to every employee in the organization?
7. Do you admit mistakes in your department (or company) and report them publicly.
8. Do you encourage whistle-blowers?

Some of the questions are easier to answer than others, but if any of them made you cringe, your transparency needs work. (A transparent leader would have answered no to the first three and yes to the rest of the questions on that questionnaire.

43-(The Transparent Leader: How to Build a Great Company through Straight Talk, Openness, and Accountability. Herb Baum, The Transparent Company, pg 6-7. Harper Business Press, 2004)

Basic Words of Communication

THEORY X
&
THEORY Y

o o o
What is it?

A concept presented by Douglas McGregor in The Human Side of Enterprise. Theory X describes a worker who is lazy and money oriented and produces only because of the presence of an authoritarian supervisor. Theory Y describes a worker who is eager to work, is motivated by various means, and requires a flexible, human-relations style of leadership.

How does it apply?

Theory X and Theory Y's association with culture change in this instance actually falls under the topic of stereotyping. I think many of us are quick to label specific cultures under Theory X and others under Theory Y based on our own worldviews. The African American culture is many times linked to Theory X behaviors because of unknown understandings attached to that culture. Asian Americans are linked to Theory Y based on understandings of that culture. These distinctions are made even though there may be no more of an understanding of either culture.

The ABC's of Diversity:

Where there negative stereotypes or assumptions learned in your life based only on what another biased person indicated?

○ ○ ○

Beliefs in which a person or social group have an emotional investment, that suggest one way of acting or being is preferred to another.

○ ○ ○

The overall perspective from which one sees and interprets the world and, the belief structure from which one makes determinations such as what is right and wrong

157

Basic Words of Communication

Research
Questionnaire:

"HOW CULTURALLY SENSITIVE IS YOUR ORGANIZATION'S EGO?"

Respecting others is an important factor for all cultures. We need to better understand our cultural biases and why we do the things we do. We should also utilize whatever research available, past and present, to further explain our worldviews, and how those worldviews affect our ability to be more or less cross-culturally competent. With this direction in mind, let's use Sigmund Freud's research to investigate the organization's "Ego."

The ABC's of Diversity:

Freud established the theory that unconscious motives control much of one's behavior. According to his Psychoanalytical Theory, he further explains that "the 'Id' is an important part of our personality because it allows us to get our needs met. The "Ego" understands that other people have needs and desires and its job is to meet those demands. The "Super-Ego" is our conscience and dictates between what's right and wrong."

When analyzing the differences between the three, the Ego probably has another tremendous responsibility. If, in fact, you agree with Freud's research, it would probably be the Ego's job to understand the needs and desires of others and to fulfill those needs. Therefore, it would be a justifiable assumption that a non-inclusive environment seeking a higher level of cultural sensitivity would fall under the Ego's umbrella of responsibility.

A workplace struggling to acknowledge respectful attitudes indicates there may be a major void in the mindsets of "those other" employees. To measure the importance of such attitudes, organizations need to make sure the "magnitude of the gap" between truth and perception is well understood and well documented.

"How Culturally Sensitive is Your Organization's Ego" is a confidential opportunity for honest workplace feedback to be recorded and evaluated without fear of retribution to the respondents. The instrument is designed to capture

Basic Words of Communication

The ABC's of Diversity:

individual perceptions of workplace truths about leadership, accountability, and commitment. It differs from the earlier mentioned Cross-Cultural Competence instrument in that it measures "the cultural sensitivity of the organization" where the other concentrates on personal worldviews only. Take the time to respond to the following research questions. They are designed to acknowledge the truth about your workplace and to validate an accurate pulse of a specific environment.

Please remember. As you respond to each question, the basis for this instrument is to measure the perception of your organization's ego? (i.e., Does your organization mandate policies of inclusiveness just to be politically correct for the sake of its bottom-line? Or, does the organization truly seek cultural equality in the workplace?) Your responses are strictly confidential.

<u>Research Questionnaire:</u>

(1) Is your leadership's level of cultural sensitivity based on a theory of denial? (i.e., acknowledging or responding to culturally sensitive issues as though they do not exist?)

Yes?_____ No?_____

Comments:_____

_____

_____

Basic Words of Communication

The ABC's of Diversity:

(2) Have you ever heard authority figures refer to others in the organization as "you people or those people?"

Yes?_____ No?_____

*Comments:*_____

_____

_____

(4) Are your leaders sincere when they express feelings about establishing a respectful workplace?

Yes?_____ No?_____

*Comments:*_____

_____

_____

(4) When addressing problems in the workplace that involve some degree of cultural difference, do decision-makers tend to deliver a fair solution?

Yes?_____ No?_____ Indecisive?_____

*Comments:*_____

_____

_____

Basic Words of Communication

The ABC's of Diversity:

(5) Do you think your leadership understands the cultural truths about the organization?

Yes?_____ No?_____ Indecisive?_____

Comments:_____

_____

_____

(5) Is there a sense of "anxiety" in the faces and voices of leaders when they interact in multi-cultural environments?

Yes?_____ No?_____ Indecisive?_____

What would be an example of anxiety:_____

_____

_____

(6) Is there and "open door" policy with leadership where you can sit down and "honestly" talk about cultural differences without being negatively labeled?

Yes?_____ No?_____ Indecisive?_____

What would be an example of anxiety:_____

_____

_____

Basic Words of Communication

The ABC's of Diversity:

(7) Is there an overall perception that recruitment and retention policies and practices are based primarily on cultural differences?

Yes?_____ No?_____ Indecisive?_____

Comments:_____

_____

_____

(8) Do you think your organization's diversity and inclusion mandates are real or just smoke screens of political correctness?

Yes?_____ No?_____ Indecisive?_____

Comments:_____

_____

_____

(9) Is your leadership held accountable at all levels?

Yes?_____ No?_____ Indecisive?_____

Comments:_____

_____

_____

The ABC's of Diversity:

(10) Are diversity mandates only for lower level employees?

     *Yes?*_____   *No?*_____   *Indecisive?*_____

*Comments:*_____

_____

_____

(11) Does the organization recognize its lack of cultural respect and sensitivity but just don't know what to do about it?

     *Yes?*_____   *No?*_____   *Indecisive?*_____

*Comments:*_____

_____

_____

(12) Executives understand the necessity of sensitivity training – but only as it applies to "others"?

     *Yes?*_____   *No?*_____   *Indecisive?*_____

*Comments:*_____

_____

_____

Basic Words of Communication

The ABC's of Diversity:

(13) Do you think that, although the organization seeks inclusion, it wants to do so without changing the present status quo?

Yes?_____ No?_____ Indecisive?_____

Comments:_____
_____
_____

(14) Does your workforce resemble the changing face of America?

Yes?_____ No?_____ Indecisive?_____

Comments:_____
_____
_____

(15) Is there a lack of respect found "within" similar cultural communities at your workplace?

Yes?_____ No?_____ Indecisive?_____

Comments:_____
_____
_____

The ABC's of Diversity:

(16) Are there "unofficial" rules and regulations not written but definitely "implied?"

Yes?_____ No?_____ Indecisive?_____

Comments:_____
_____
_____

(17) Do you think personnel evaluations are influenced by ethnicity?

Yes?_____ No?_____ Indecisive?_____

Comments:_____
_____
_____

(18) Are mid-level managers pressured to choose between production numbers and being socially correct?

Yes?_____ No?_____ Indecisive?_____

Comments:_____
_____
_____

Basic Words of Communication

The ABC's of Diversity:

(19) Is the service or product you provide affected by demographic changes?

Yes?_____ No?_____ Indecisive?_____

Comments:_____
_____
_____

(20) Does leadership ask for your insights on how to make the workplace a better place?

Yes?_____ No?_____ Indecisive?_____

Comments:_____
_____
_____

(21) Does the organization really want change?

Yes?_____ No?_____ Indecisive?_____

Comments:_____
_____
_____

The ABC's of Diversity:

(22) Do you foresee a long tenure at your current workplace?

      *Yes?*_____   *No?*_____   *Indecisive?*_____

*Comments:*_____
_____
_____

(23) Does freedom of speech on "culturally sensitive issues" carry a huge price in your workplace arena?

      *Yes?*_____   *No?*_____   *Indecisive?*_____

*Comments:*_____
_____
_____

(24) Do you have confidence that the current leadership can lead your organization into an era of "respect and inclusion."

      *Yes?*_____   *No?*_____   *Indecisive?*_____

*Comments:*_____
_____
_____

The ABC's of Diversity:

(25) Can you do anything to enhance your organization's diversity initiatives?

Yes?_____ No?_____ Indecisive?_____

Comments:_____
_____
_____

For results and analysis please visit our website @ LanierDiversityConsultants.com. Follow the Research Questionnaire instructions and record your responses confidentially.

I SINCERELY THANK EACH AND EVERY ONE OF YOU FOR YOUR SUPPORT!

I ALSO THANK EVERY REFERENCE USED TO MAKE THIS RESEARCH A RICHER LEARNING EXPERIENCE!

- Leon T. Lanier

Content Suggestion Box

This property seeks to sustain a high level of inclusiveness by listing diversity-related terms applicable to a multitude of workplace environments.

Content suggestions for the 2nd Edition of "The ABC's of Diversity" are eagerly requested. Please go to LanierDiversityConsultant.com and follow the link to the Content Suggestion Box to complete the suggestion process.

Your input is a not only a necessity but a mandate.

LDC…

The ABC's of Diversity:

BIBLIOGRAPHY

∘ ∘∘∘

1-(Excerpt from the Intercultural Development Inventory Manual by Dr. Mitch Hammer and Dr. Milton Bennett, 1998). pg 2;

2-(Driving Fear out of the Workplace: Creating the High Trust – High Performance Organization by Kathleen Ryan and Daniel Oestreich, pg 131). Pg 10

3-(taken from the Intercultural Development Inventory Manual by Dr. Mitch Hammer and Dr. Milton Bennett, 1998). Pg 11.

4-(Kathleen Ryan & Daniel Ostreich; Driving Fear out of the Workplace: Creating a High Trust High Performance Organization; Second Edition, pge 129; Jossey-Bass, 1998.) Pg 12.

5-(taken from Diversity Success Strategies, Chapter 2, pg 34, written by Norma-Carr Ruffino, Butterworth/Heinemann Publishers, 1999) Pg 16.

6-(Jim Collins, Good to Great, Chapter 4, pg 78, Harper Business Press, 2001) Pg 27.

7-(excerpt from The New Mainstream, Chapter 1, pg 21, written by Guy Garcia, Harper Collins Publisher, 2004) Pg. 29.

8-(The New Mainstream: How the Multicultural Consumer is Transforming American Business, Introduction pg 10, written by Guy Garcia, Harper Collins Publishers, 2004) Pg 33;

9-(Stephen R. Covey's The 8th Habit: From Effectiveness to Greatness, chapter 7, pg 132, Free Press/Simon & Schuster) Pg 35;

10-(Talent Management Handbook, Lance Berger and Dorothy Berger, Chapter 27, pg 297, Integrating Coaching, Training, and Development with Talent Management (Helen Krewson), McGraw Hill Publishers, 2004) Pg 37;

Basic Words of Communication

The ABC's of Diversity:

11-(taken from Diversity Success Strategies, Chapter 2, pg 46, written by Norma-Carr Ruffino, Butterworth/Heinemann Publishers, 1999) pg 40;

12-(Building a Reservoir of High Potential Women and Diverse Groups, Leon T Lanier, Sr., The Talent Management Handbook by Berger and Berger, Chapter 10, page 273, Mcgraw-Hill, 2004.) Pg 42;

13-(Excerpts from "The Medici Effect: Breakthrough Insights at the Intersection of Ideas, Concepts, and Cultures. Frans Johansson, Introduction pg 2, Harvard Business School Press, 2004.) pg 44;

14-(taken from Diversity Success Strategies, Chapter 2, pg 18, written by Norma-Carr Ruffino, Butterworth/Heinemann Publishers, 1999) pg 63;

15-(Excerpt from the Intercultural Development Inventory Manual by Dr. Mitch Hammer and Dr. Milton Bennett, 1998). Pg 67;

16-(Excerpt from the Intercultural Development Inventory Manual by Dr. Mitch Hammer and Dr. Milton Bennett, 1998). Pg 68;

17-(Norma-Carr Ruffino, Diversity Success Strategies, Chapter 10, pg 240, Butterworth/Hieneman, 1999) pg 71;

18-(Norma-Carr Ruffino, Diversity Success Strategies, Chapter 2, pg 65, Butterworth/Heinemann Press, 1999) pg 73;

19-(Kathleen Ryan & Daniel Ostreich; Driving Fear out of the Workplace: Creating a High Trust High Performance Organization; Second Edition, pge 209; Chapter 12, Discuss the Undiscussables; Jossey-Bass, 1998.) pg 64;

20-(The Harvard Business Review on Corporate Ethics. Ethics in Practice by Kenneth R. Andrews, pge 71-72, Harvard Business School Press, 2003) pg 82;

21-(taken from Diversity Success Strategies, Chapter 3, pg 67, written by Norma-Carr Ruffino, Butterworth/Heinemann Publishers, 1999) pg 84;

Basic Words of Communication

The ABC's of Diversity:

22-(Taken from the Intercultural Development Inventory Manual Research by Dr. Mitchell Hammer and Dr. Milton Bennett, 1998, The Developmental Model of Intercultural Sensitivity (DMIS). Pg 85;

23-(The 21 Irrefutable Laws of Leadership, John C. Maxwell, Chapter 2: The Laws of Influence, pg 14, Nelson Business Press, 1998.) pg 91;

24-(The Harvard Business Review on Corporate Ethics. Guidelines for Ethical Leadership by Thomas Donaldson, pge 131, Harvard Business School Press, 2003) pg 94;

25-(Gutsy Leadership: A Common Sense Workbook on Leadership Development, Leon T. Lanier, Sr., Renaissance Publishers, Inc, 2003) pg 95;

*26-*Gutsy Leadership: A Common Sense Workbook on Leadership Development, Leon T. Lanier, Sr., Renaissance Publishers, Inc. pg 51, 2003) pg 96;

27-(Kathleen Ryan & Daniel Ostreich; Driving Fear out of the Workplace: Creating a High Trust High Performance Organization; Second Edition, pge 190; Chapter 11, Reduce Ambiguous Behavior; Jossey-Bass, 1998) pg 100;

28-(Driving Fear Out of The Workplace, Kathleen Ryan and Daniel Oestreich, Chapter 16, pg 294, Jossey-Bass Publishers, 1998) pg 103;

29-(Gutsy Leadership: a Common Sense Workbook on Leadership Development, Leon T. Lanier, Renaissance Publishers, 2003) pg 107;

30-(The 8th Habit from Effectiveness to Greatness, Stephen R. Covey, pg 98, Free Press of Simon and Schuster, inc, 2004.) pg 114;

31-(taken from the Intercultural Development Inventory Manual by Dr. Mitch Hammer and Dr. Milton Bennett, 1998). Pg 118;

32-(taken from Diversity Success Strategies, Chapter 6, pg 128, written by Norma-Carr Ruffino, Butterworth/Heinemann Publishers, 1999) pg 120;

33-(Taken from Diversity Success Strategies, Chapter , pg 156, written by Norma-Carr Ruffino, Butterworth/Heinemann Publishers, 1999) pg 121;

Basic Words of Communication

The ABC's of Diversity:

34-(taken from Diversity Success Strategies, Chapter 8, pg 184, written by Norma-Carr Ruffino, Butterworth/Heinemann Publishers, 1999) pg 123;

35-(taken from Diversity Success Strategies, Chapter 9, pg 211, written by Norma-Carr Ruffino, Butterworth/Heinemann Publishers, 1999) pg 124;

36-(Gutsy Leadership: a Common Sense Workbook on Leadership Development, Leon T. Lanier, pg 30-32, Renaissance Publishers, 2003) pg 128;

37-(taken from Diversity Success Strategies, Chapter 3, pg 66, written by Norma-Carr Ruffino, Butterworth/Heinemann Publishers, 1999) pg 133;

38-(Gutsy Leadership: A Common Sense Workbook on Leadership Development, 1st Edition, Leon T. Lanier, Sr., Chapter IV, pg 45, renaissance Publishers, 2002) pg 134;

39-(taken from Diversity Success Strategies, Chapter 3, pg 66, written by Norma-Carr Ruffino, Butterworth/Heinemann Publishers, 1999) Pg. 137;

40-(taken from the Intercultural Development Inventory Manuel by Dr. Mitchell Hammer and Dr, Milton Bennett, 1998. Pg 139;

41-(Stephen R. Covey, The 8th Habit, Chapter 7, The Voice of Influence, pg 132, 142, Simon and Schuster, 2005) pg 142;

42-(taken from Diversity Success Strategies, Chapter 3, pg 66, written by Norma-Carr Ruffino, Butterworth/Heinemann Publishers, 1999) pg 143;

43-(The Tipping Point, Malcolm Gladwell, Chapter 1, pg 28, Back Bay Books/Little, Brown & Company, 2002) pg 153;

44-(The Transparent Leader: How to Build a Great Company through Straight Talk, Openness, and Accountability. Herb Baum, The Transparent Company, pg 6-7. Harper Business Press, 2004) pg 155;

Basic Words of Communication

The ABC's of Diversity:

BIOGRAPHY:

Leon T. Lanier, Sr.
CEO - Lanier Diversity Consultants, Inc.

Leon T. Lanier, Sr., M.Ed., is Chief Executive Officer of a new entity - Lanier Diversity Consultants, Inc. (LDC) specializing in developing diversity and inclusion strategies that increase organizational successes within the workplace. Mr. Lanier's previous 5 years of experience as Chief Operating Officer and Senior Lead Consultant for The Winters Group, Inc of Metropolitan Washington, DC, included management of total company operations, design of diversity curricula, and conducting diversity-related educational conferences for a wide range of national and international clientele.

Mr. Lanier successfully introduced and directed a year-long diversity process for more than 10,000 Eastman Kodak Company employees in Rochester, New York addressing "diversity awareness" in the workplace. He developed and established Diversity Councils and many diversity initiatives at major corporations such as Hewitt Associates of Chicago, IL; HCA Healthcare of Nashville, TN; Interep Radio of New York, NY; FedEx of Pittsburgh, PA; and, Exxon Mobil of Rochester, NY. Other client relationships include Nationwide Insurance of Columbus, OH, the University of Michigan Institute for Social Research in Anne Arbor, MI, and Baltimore Gas & Electric Company in Baltimore, MD.

Internationally, Mr. Lanier presented diversity and inclusion strategies for consideration by the various Ministers of Brazil, the CEOs of IBM, Xerox, and the World Bank in South America. In February 2004, he successfully conducted the inaugural TWG-Brazil Diversity Conference in Salvador, Bahia, Brazil addressing topics on diversity and inclusion. In August of 2004, he was a guest at the World Diversity Conference for Human Resources Leaders in Rio de Janeiro, Brazil and is a Founding Member and speaker at the World Diversity Leadership Summit held in Prague,

177

Basic Words of Communication

The ABC's of Diversity:

Czech Republic each year. Mr. Lanier has also worked in a leadership development capacity with St. Thomas and St. Croix of the USVI.

Prior to his work with The Winters Group, Mr. Lanier was the lead consultant for Wilbourn and Associates of Philadelphia, PA. Mr. Lanier's expertise spans across development and delivery of executive business skills to conduct instructional seminars to AT&T middle management across 25 cities in the United States. Mr. Lanier has been involved in organizational workforce development for more than 30 years. He worked with the FBI and developed and delivered training curricula for the Metropolitan Police Department of Washington, D.C. in the 1970's and '80's. He was an official national spokesperson on Child Abuse and Neglect issues as a member of the Presidential Task Force under the Nixon administration.

Lanier Diversity Consultants, Inc. officially announced its entry into the national and international diversity arena in January 2005. Since that time, it has been retained by Interep Radio of New York City, united to form a consulting status with US Cellular of Knoxville, TN and Tulsa, OK, subcontracted to interact with the United States Secret Service of Washington, DC, and secured representation of the New York/New Jersey Minority Development Supplier Program in New York City as its GlobalSource Ambassador with regional and international diversity responsibilities. I truly thank The Winters Group for my personal development and to those clients who see the value in organizational strategies LDC, Inc. can deliver in the future.

Mr. Lanier received a Criminal Law Degree from the American University of Washington, DC and Bachelor and Master Degrees in Adult Education from the University of Cincinnati. He has authored and published many books and articles including a recent contribution in the August 2004 **"Talent Management Handbook"** entitled **"Corporate Succession Planning for Women and Minorities"** (McGraw Hill) with outstanding review by the Harvard Business Review in September 2004. Other works include **"The ABC's of Diversity: Basic Workplace Communication"** – a reference that addresses diversity

Basic Words of Communication

The ABC's of Diversity:

communication skills in the workplace; **"Gutsy Leadership: a Common Sense Workbook on Leadership Development"**; **"Caveman Psychology: Men Understanding Women"**; and, the upcoming article in the May 2005 issue of Profiles in Diversity Journal entitled, **"The Value of Being Cross Culturally Competent."**

Lanier Diversity Consultants, Inc. (LDC) specializes in Diversity and Inclusion Strategies, Focus Group Research and Data Collection Processes, augmented with the support of Theatre-based Education Workshops. As a Certified IDI (Intercultural Development Inventory) Specialist, LDC, Inc. is available to conduct and deliver IDI assessments and feedback sessions for a wide array of organizational leaders and individual contributors.

For Further Info:

Consulting Services
Workshops
Speaking Engagements
Book Orders

Contact:
Leon T. Lanier, Sr.
703–863–2772
Laniersr497@aol.com
LanierDiversityConsultants.com

Basic Words of Communication